Contents

Introduction

The Handbook of Cat Breeds

The Handbook of Cat Breeds

Maria Costantino

ISLAND BOOKS

This edition published in 2003 by
S. WEBB & Son (Distributors) LTD
Telford Place, Pentraeth Road,
Menai Bridge,
Isle of Anglesey, LL59 5RW

© 2003 D&S Books Ltd

D&S Books Ltd
Kerswell,
Parkham Ash, Bideford
Devon, England
EX39 5PR

e-mail us at:-
enquiries@dsbooks.fsnet.co.uk

This edition printed 2003

ISBN 1-85657-61-5

DS0079 Cat Breed

Creative Director: Sarah King
Editor: Daniel Green
Project editor: Sally MacEachern
Photographer: Paul Forrester
Designer: Axis Design Editions
Map images © Cadmium systems

Fonts used in this book: Futura,
Akzidenz Grotesk and Gill Sans

Printed in China

1 3 5 7 9 10 8 6 4 2

FROM WILD CAT...

A Tiger in your Living Room?

'When I play with my cat, who knows whether she isn't

amusing herself with me more than I am with her?'

So wrote the French moralist and essayist, Michel de Montaigne (1533–92) in his *Essais* of 1580. We may well have domesticated cats into a world where they depend on humans, nevertheless, cats are not – nor will ever be – our property. Like Montaigne, most cat owners will readily admit that it is, in fact, their cat that owns them! While domestic cats are content to accept the food, shelter and affection we provide, a cat will always live according to its feline instincts and needs.

Around 50 million years ago, during the Cenozoic era (the 'Age of Recent Life') at the twilight of the age of the dinosaurs, creodonts, the ancient ancestors of the modern cat appeared. The creodonts would eventually give way to miacids – larger-brained, carnivorous mammals from which descend canids (including dogs) and viverrids (the family of small carnivorous mammals including civets, mongooses, palm cats and genets). The first true cat, the *Pseudoailurus*, was the ancestor of the *Smilodon*, the famous Sabre-toothed Tiger, which was around 183 cm (6 ft) long with 20 cm- (8 in-) long upper canine teeth, and whose remains have been found in North America. A similar cat, the *Megantereon*, which was found in Northern Africa, India and around the Mediterranean countries, was the ancestor of the lions, cheetahs and lynxes which were widespread throughout Europe.

...TO KITTY-CAT.

IN THE WILD.

The whole cat family is very closely related: both the biggest cat, the Siberian Tiger, which can weigh as much as 383 kg (845 lb), and the smallest domestic 'moggie' are classified in the same genus – *Felis*. Australia and Antarctica are the only continents that do not have native species of cats, but wild cats can be found throughout the rest of the world.

Zoologists are not certain from exactly which of the 39 species of wild cats our domestic cats are descended. *Felis sylvestris*, the European Wild Cat, is a good contender, as it looks remarkably like a domestic tabby – only a little larger and with a rounded tip to its tail. The European Wild Cat is now known only in northern parts of Scotland and in the more remote parts of northern Europe, but was once common and ranged throughout Britain and the forested areas of continental Europe. But it appears that *Felis lybica*, the African Wild Cat, is the more likely progenitor. Even the word 'cat' suggests this African link, as the root word may be the Arabic *quttah* – which does sound a little like 'kitty'!

The first record of cats living alongside humans is some 8000 years ago. In 1983, an archaeological dig at the Neolithic site of Khirokitia in southern Cyprus uncovered a feline jawbone. Early settlers on the island must have taken domesticated cats with them since Cyprus had no wild cats. It seems likely that the domesticated Cypriot Cat came originally from Egypt because, unlike the European Wild Cat, the African Wild Cat is quite easy to tame.

DOMESTIC CATS SHARE THE SAME BASIC INSTINCTS AS WILD CATS.

ANCIENT EGYPT PROVIDES THE EARLIEST REPRESENTATIONS OF CATS.

Cats are, however, one of the more recent animals to be domesticated. Long before cats appeared in the home, dogs had been man's companions. Whereas dogs are pack animals, cats hunt alone and so had nothing to gain by joining forces with the prehistoric hunter. Later, when man began to keep flocks of animals that had to be moved to summer and winter pastures, dogs were used to herd and guard animals. But such a migratory life was of no interest for the territorial cat.

By around 3000 BC, when man had settled down and started to grow crops and store grain, then there was a partnership to be made. Grain stores attract vermin such as mice and rats. Man was now offering cats a convenient and well-stocked hunting ground as well as cosy, warm habitations,

in return for cats providing the very valuable service of protecting man's grain stores. Not surprising then that the earliest representations of cats are to be found in wall paintings from ancient Egypt – a land dependent on the grain harvests of the Nile Valley.

The earliest Egyptian painting of a cat is a mural in a tomb dating from around 2600 BC that shows a cat wearing a collar. Whether this cat was domesticated is uncertain, but by 2000 BC in ancient Egypt, the cat was being worshipped as a deity. A number of gods and goddesses took feline forms such as the great Sun God, Ra (no doubt because cats always enjoy the heat of the sun!) and Mafdet, who was represented as a snake-killing cat (no doubt a very valuable asset in a land

9

CATS PLAYED A VITAL ROLE IN THE AGRARIAN ECONOMY OF EGYPT AND WERE WORSHIPPED AS GODS.

where deadly snakes lurk!) It was however with Bast, or Bastet, the cat-headed goddess of fertility, that cats were most associated. In the city of Bubastis on the Lower Nile, the centre of the Bast cult, was a great temple dedicated to the goddess. In the temple grounds lived the shrine's cats, guarded by priests who also watched the cats' behaviour to see if the goddess was 'speaking'.

Each year the city and temple celebrated with a great festival in Bast's honour. These celebrations – many of which were associated with fertility rites and proved quite shocking for visitors in later centuries – continued right through the Christian era until AD 392 when the Byzantine Emperor Theodosius suppressed the cult.

By around 1800 BC, it appears that Egyptian cats were domesticated in the modern sense of the word. Tomb paintings, such as the splendid example (now in the British Museum in London) from the tomb of a scribe and counter of grain called Nebamun, dating from the New Kingdom (c. 1567–1085 BC), also show cats – this time one specially trained to retrieve water fowl hunted in the river marshes.

Because they were so highly thought of, Egyptian owners ceremonially mummified their dead cats and took their bodies to the city of Bubastis for burial. Kittens – probably because of their size – appear to have been dipped in preserving chemicals and wrapped carefully in linen. Their

remains are little more than tiny piles of dust and bone fragments, although some were encased in tiny bronze caskets, often surmounted by the figure of a cat.

Adult cats, however, were treated much more elaborately in preparation for the 'afterlife' and wealthy owners took great care to wrap them in fine linen. Bodies were arranged with the rear legs in the seated position, the front paws stretched straight down and the tail curved to lie against the belly – posed in death as if they were alive. The body was wound in a sheet of linen and then in a cylindrical covering of braided ribbons in two colours, possibly to reproduce the colourings and markings of the fur. Covering the head was a papyrus paper mask to which were attached discs of linen, painted to represent the eyes. The nostrils and ears were fashioned from palm fronds. The preserved and bound mummy was then placed in a funerary box, often made of wood or bronze, shaped like a seated cat, and painted to make them more lifelike (or catlike).

More than 300,000 mummified cats and kittens were discovered in the 19th century in Bubastis, neatly arranged on tiers of shelves in the tunnels of an underground cemetery – a true 'catacomb'! Only a

A STATUE OF A CAT REPESENTING THE GOD BASTET.

handful remain however: some can be seen in the British Museum and other collections, but most of them had their heads slashed off and their contents spread as fertiliser on local fields. In 1889, nearly 20 tons of cat mummies were pulverised, shipped to Liverpool as fertiliser, and auctioned off at £4 per ton.

This ran contrary to the ancient Egyptians laws which severely punished anyone who deliberately harmed a cat and furthermore, strictly forbade the export of cats – alive or dead – to other countries! Nevertheless,

THE ROMANS BROUGHT CATS
BACK TO ITALY AFTER DEFEATING
CLEOPATRA'S ARMY IN 30 BC.

some were obviously smuggled out of the country for images of cats began to appear on coins and vases in Greece and Italy. When Egypt became a province of the Roman Empire in 30 BC following the defeat of Queen Cleopatra's army, the Romans took Egyptian cats back with them to Italy.

As Roman power spread across Europe and Asia, unsurprisingly their cats went too. Remains of Roman cats have been found in Britain in places which suggest they were domestic animals. While not worshipped as a god as in Egypt, the cat in Roman times was associated with Diana, the huntress and goddess of the Moon. In the fourth century AD, the agriculturalist Palladius, wrote of the value of cats in protecting gardens from mice and moles.

Following the fall of the Roman Empire were the Dark Ages in Europe during which the Christian Church sought to establish itself and replace the many surviving pagan beliefs, and attitudes towards cats became polarised. On the one hand, many countries protected cats by law and in English convents, cats were considered suitable 'companions' for nuns. In AD 936 Hywel (Hywel Dda), Prince of Wales, set out laws determining the value of cats: a kitten, until it opened its eyes, was worth one penny, then twopence until it caught its first mouse, when its worth increased to fourpence! And, if a cat employed to guard the royal grainstores was killed, enough wheat to completely cover the cat's body was required as compensation for its unlawful death.

On the other hand, the cat was regarded by many as an agent of the devil! In the early Middle Ages, the figure of the Roman goddess Diana, the huntress associated

DURING THE MIDDLE AGES CATS BECAME ASSOCIATED WITH WITCHCRAFT, WHICH LED TO THEIR WIDESPREAD PERSECUTION.

with the moon and with cats, became transformed into Hecate, queen of the night and chief of the witches. Consequently, cats – especially black cats – became associated with the 'dark arts' of magic, which led to their widespread persecution.

Witch – and cat – persecution mania in Britain reached its peak in the mid-17th century when Matthew Hopkins, the Witchfinder General, sent hundreds of 'witches' to their death following confessions often gained under torture. Because the cat was an ideal companion for the poor and lonely – it could hunt its own food and offered purring affection to comfort their owners – religious mania and fearful superstition allowed many to misinterpret the close bond between people and their cats. The Puritan preacher John Paul published a collection of sermons on witchcraft in which he went so far as to

13

state that, 'old woman with a wrinkled face, hairy lip, squint eye, a spindle in her hand and a dog or cat at her side, is not only suspected but pronounced a witch'.

Regrettably, such attitudes were not confined only to Britain but were exported by religious zealots among the settlers in America. The most famous witchcraft trials in the New England colonies took place in 1692 in Salem, Massachusetts, where a witness claimed a cat attacked him at night as he slept after a suspected witch threatened that a 'she devil would shortly fetch him away'.

While cats were held in low esteem and often persecuted in the West, in the East, cats were held in much higher regard. In China, farmers worshipped the fertility god Li Chou in his cat form and offered ritual sacrifices to cats when the harvest was gathered. In Japan, cats were also sacred animals and today, tortoiseshell and tricolour cats are regarded as bringers of good luck.

All across the Far East cats are considered to be lucky: in Malaysia and Indonesia, it is believed that bathing a cat will bring rain! While Christianity has often seen the cat as evil, in Islam, the cat is considered to be pure. The prophet

MUSLIMS REGARD THE CAT AS 'BLESSED': MOHAMMED'S CAT WAS CALLED MUEZZA.

Mohammed is said to have cut off his shirt sleeve rather than disturb his favourite cat, Muezza, when he woke to find the cat asleep on his arm.

Cats were cited as witches' familiars in the last witch trials in both England (1712) and Scotland (1722). But cats would soon start being presented as benevolent

creatures in stories like 'Puss in Boots' and 'Dick Whittington'. Even so, it was not the end of cruelty to cats. It would not be until 1822 that the British Parliament passed the first laws protecting animals – although initially the legislation applied only to cattle and draught animals. In 1824, a meeting of animal lovers in London established the Society for the Prevention of Cruelty to Animals and in 1840, Queen Victoria added her support and patronage to the SPCA. and gave it the prefix Royal.

DESPITE DIFFERENCES IN SIZE, THE TIGER IS A CLOSE RELATIVE OF THE DOMESTIC CAT.

APPEARANCES ARE DECEPTIVE: THE PAMPERED DOMESTIC CAT STILL RETAINS MANY OF ITS NATURAL INSTINCTS.

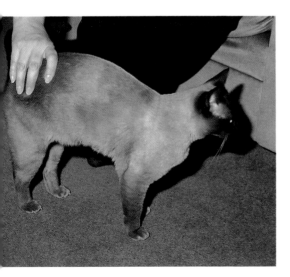

While our attitudes to cats have changed over the centuries, and many different types have appeared – there are now more than 100 different breeds recognised around the world and an infinite number of variations among the moggies – cats' natural instincts have been little modified by living with and alongside man. The sleek furred pet, gently purring in your lap or comfortably curled up in front of the fire, remains a fierce and effective predator, a close relative of the African lion and the Indian tiger. One of the most efficiently designed animals, with highly developed senses, they are also patient hunters who stalk their quarry stealthily or remain motionless until the moment comes to spring on their prey.

15

Chapter 1

Moggies and Pedigrees

While dogs have been selectively bred for centuries – not only for their looks but for their working suitability – it was only in the 19th century, with the first cat shows, that any serious attempts at planning and controlling the breeding of cats for their physical appearance began. Since then, many different patterns and colours have been developed and fixed by breeders and strict standards have been laid down by the various cat organisations to which the 100-plus breeds of cat must conform. However, not all breeds are recognised in every country or by every cat organisation.

Mongrels, moggies or alley cats, whatever you like to call them, are cats of undetermined parentage and that do not conform to breed standards. In short, their pedigree is unknown – even though their appearance may suggest that 'dad' was a particular local tom! The word 'pedigree' is misleading: all cats, whether a moggie or prize puss, have a pedigree – an ancestral history – but the term is generally used to mean a cat which is pure bred through several generations, with all its ancestors from a particular breed. Nevertheless, while some of the older breeds have their origins in myth or romance, even the exact origins of some of

TABBIES OCCUR IN PURE-BRED PEDIGREE BREEDS AS WELL AS BEING THE MOST NUMEROUS OF THE NON-PEDIGREE 'MOGGIES'.

the more modern breeds are not easy to trace and are a matter of great debate.

Because of cats' dominant genes there are probably more tabby cats among the moggies than any other colour, and more short-haired non-pedigree moggies than long-haired ones. In general, moggies tend to be 'cobbies' – stockily built, with round paws. Their faces are by no means less expressive and appealing than their well-bred cousins, likewise, a long-haired, non-pedigree puss is no less graceful than a pure bred Persian! It's not surprising then that cats of every size, pattern and colour are the world's most popular urban pet.

Pedigree Cats and Breed Registries

Although it appears that cats shows were held in the 16th century – one is recorded at St. Giles' Fair in Winchester, England in 1598 – it was more likely that they were showcase-and-sales for good mousers! In 1871, Harrison Weir organised the first formal cat show at the Crystal Palace in London. Weir, who was also one of the three judges of the 160 exhibits, also devised the 'standard of points' for all the breeds shown. In 1887, the National Cat Club was formed in Britain – with Weir as its first president. Although the standards have changed over the years, Weirs' basic arrangement of the cat show remained pretty constant. In some breeds the standards are common worldwide, while in other breeds the standards vary from country to country. The standards set by the different

WHILE STANDARDS HAVE CHANGED OVER THE YEARS, THE BASIC ARRANGEMENT OF THE CAT SHOW HAS REMAINED CONSTANT.

cat associations are for ideal appearance – body shape, colour and pattern – although recently, temperament has also been taken into account by show judges.

In North America, the first cat show to attract serious attention was organised by James T. Hyde at Madison Square Garden, New York in 1895, where a Maine Coon was judged champion – even though the breed itself would not be officially

THE CHAMPION OF AMERICA'S FIRST CAT SHOW IN 1895 WAS A MAINE COON.

THE HAIRLESS SPHYNX IS CURRENTLY RECOGNISED ONLY BY THE TICA.

recognised in the US until 1967! – and in 1896, the American Cat Club became the first US registry.

The largest of the registries of pedigree cats today is the CFA (Cat Fancier's Association) which was founded in 1906 and has affiliated clubs in the United States and Canada, South America, Europe and Japan. The CFA's registering policy has often been described as 'purist', allowing only certain colours of breeds to be included in its registry.

A little less strict is the GCCF, Britain's Governing Council of the Cat Fancy, formed in 1910 with affiliations in South Africa, Australia and New Zealand.

Across Europe, many registries belong to the FIFé (Fédération Internationale Féline), which began in 1949 and now claims to be the largest cat club in the world.

The most liberal and experimental of all the registries is the TICA (The International Cat Association), founded in 1979 in North America. Because each association has different rules for inclusion and exclusion, some breeds – and only some colours or patterns of that breed – may be only officially recognised by one organisation. For example, while the 'hairless' Sphynx, the 'newer' bicolour combinations of some Oriental breeds, or the 'dwarf' Munchkin are all recognised as breeds by the TICA, these cats remain excluded from other registries. Each country's association also registers kittens, the transfer of ownership and approves the calendar of cat-show dates.

Categories of Breed

If the domestic non-pedigree cat is not included – although cat shows often have a class for these where judgement is based on looks and condition – there are seven different categories of recognised breed:

Longhairs of Persian type

Longhairs of non-Persian type (e.g. the Maine Coon), where the only factor that these breeds have in common is their long hair

British and American Shorthairs

Burmese

Siamese

Oriental Shorthairs (usually Siamese in shape and size but not displaying the restricted coat pattern of the Siamese breed – genetically these cats have what is termed the 'Himalayan factor')

Other Shorthairs (e.g. the Rex, Mau and Abyssinian), those not fitting into the other shorthair groups

Chapter 2
Feline Facts

The Anatomy of a Cat

'Cats, no less liquid than their shadows,

Offer no angles to the wind.

They slip, diminished, neat, through loopholes,

Less than themselves'.

Cats, A.S.J. Tessimond (1934)

BALANCING ACT: CATS ARE AS AGILE AS TIGHTROPE WALKERS.

FEW OBSTACLES WILL DETER A CAT.

Just watching how smoothly a cat moves, how powerfully it can leap and pounce, how surefooted it is as it tightrope-walks along the top of garden fences and how intelligent and sensitive it is to every stimulus, makes us aware of how beautifully designed it is.

A cat's skeleton is made up of about 250 bones – depending on the breed, it may have more or fewer bones in the tail – linked by 517 muscles, which, in the legs and loins, neck and shoulders, are exceptionally strong, giving cats their powerful spring and the strength to strike down their prey. Their forelegs can turn in almost any direction, their heads can rotate through almost 180 degrees and their backbones are extremely flexible and strong.

The function of the cat's tail is something of a mystery – cats themselves seem at times to be both bemused and amused by them. Many cats seem to make a question mark out of their tail as though quizzing their owners on this ancient mystery, while even elderly cats can be quite surprised by the sight of their own tail and will chase it round for a minute or two! The cat's tail is not used for holding onto anything and it doesn't

NOTE THE FLEXIBILITY OF THE CAT'S BACKBONE.

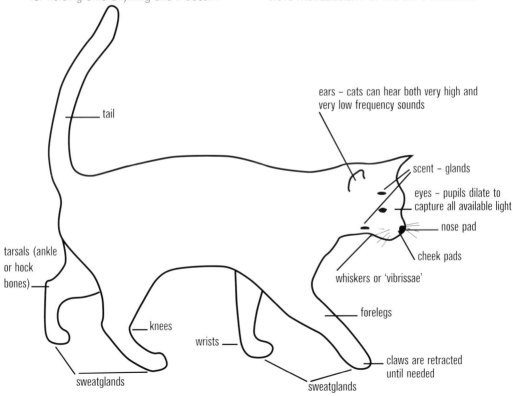

tail

ears – cats can hear both very high and very low frequency sounds

scent – glands

eyes – pupils dilate to capture all available light

nose pad

cheek pads

whiskers or 'vibrissae'

tarsals (ankle or hock bones)

knees

wrists

forelegs

claws are retracted until needed

sweatglands

sweatglands

23

STRONG LEGS AND A FLEXIBLE BACK ALLOW THE CAT TO 'PERFORM' A VARIETY OF POSTURES.

AN AVERAGE CAT WILL SNOOZE FOR BETWEEN 16 AND 18 HOURS A DAY.

really aid balance since Manx cats manage quite well without one – even if they are not first-class climbers – and other cats, who have lost their tails, adapt quite easily to active life without a tail. Nevertheless, cats' tails are very sensitive to touch, and they do puff up magnificently when unwelcome visitors dare to cross their path!

The cat's sense of balance and its ability to twist its body and reorient itself during a fall to make a level landing was once thought to be dependent on the structure of the inner ear – interestingly they don't suffer from seasickness like dogs or humans, which would account for why cats went to sea as ship's cats! However, experiments conducted on a 15-year-old white cat that had been deaf since birth suggested that

the inner ear was not the only contributing factor. When this deaf cat was dropped (safely on to a mattress to protect it from injury) it still managed to twist and right itself but, when blindfolded, not only could he not correct his body during the fall, he was very slow to right himself when he had landed. It seems that a cat's sight and its ability to register its relationship with the horizon line play some part in this 'self-righting' skill. But if a cat is not wide awake, or if it falls from a great height, then the impact can be enough to injure them – their jaws are particularly vulnerable to injury if they should strike the floor.

While agile, lithe and powerful, a cat's chest capacity is quite small, which means that its heart is small and its stamina limited. Consequently, bursts of great activity are extremely tiring and to recover from their exertions, cats must follow up

ALTHOUGH WE FEED DOMESTIC CATS REGULARLY, THEIR DIGESTIVE ORGANS ARE COMPARATIVELY LARGE, ENABLING THEM TO FEAST OR FAST.

with long (often very long!) periods of rest. On average, cats will happily sleep for between 16 and 18 hours each day. But don't let this slumber fool you – during this time, cats' senses remain ever alert and their brains active!

The small chest area allows for comparatively larger digestive organs to be accommodated, enabling cats to alternate between gorging on a kill and periods of leanness or fasting. Even though we feed our pets regularly, the digestive systems of domestic cats remain the same as their wild cousins!

Paws and Claws

Cats don't walk on their feet, but on their toes – their ankle joints are half-way up their legs. Most cats have five toes on each foreleg, and four toes on each hind leg, but polydactylism (having extra toes) is not uncommon. Polydactylism in cats is caused by a genetic mutation. In large cat populations, such mutations typically vanish after a few generations but, in isolated cat populations, mutations have a greater chance of survival. In Boston, Massachusetts and Halifax, Nova Scotia in Canada, polydactyl cats are common. When cats were first introduced to these regions by settlers, there were very few native cats with which to interbreed and breed out the mutation. Polydactyl cats, therefore, represented a large percentage of a small gene pool.

These feline digits, or fingers and toes, are not developed like ours but that does not mean that cats are not as dextrous as us! The front paws are very versatile: prey (or toys) can be firmly held down with them, they can pat, pummel and punch, and they can scoop up with them as well! Arthur, the white cat, and TV advertising star, demonstrated this technique perfectly to eat his favourite tinned food! Many cats are

THE FLESHY PAW PADS ABSORB IMPACT AND NOISE, ENABLING CATS TO WALK SILENTLY.

AN ADULT CAT'S CLAWS ARE RETRACTABLE. THEY HELP CATS TO GRIP PREY AND CLIMB TREES.

expert anglers, a skill noted by the great naturalist Charles Darwin. They use a 'dip and flip' technique – one paw scoops out the fish from the water and then the poor fish is flipped over the shoulder onto the ground, well away from the water, where it can then be pounced upon with both paws.

The fleshy paw pads under cats' feet absorb shock and act as noise inhibitors allowing cats to tip-toe silently, but they are also the site of sweat glands, which allow cats to leave their scent when they scratch a tree – or your furniture. While the rear paws are somewhat less flexible, they are still very strong and in fights can deliver series of strong 'kicks'. The claws not only help cats to grip while traversing slippery surfaces and enable them to climb trees, they are also lethal weapons.

FRONT PAWS CAN BE USED TO PUMMEL AND PUNCH.

A SCRATCHING POST ALLOWS CATS TO EXERCISE THEIR FELINE INSTINCTS WITHOUT DAMAGING THE FURNITURE.

The claws of adult cats retract into the sheaths, which not only protects them but softens the footfalls. In kittens – and Siamese cats in particular – the claws are not fully retractable and you can hear their claws click-clicking when they walk across hard surfaces!

Cats' paws also double as brushes and combs. While its flexible body structure allows it to bend and stretch to reach almost every part of its body with its tongue, the head and neck are out of reach. These are cleaned by moistening the paws and scrubbing with them.

AFTER A GOOD SNOOZE, COMES A GOOD STRETCH. THE FRONT LEGS ARE USUALLY STRETCHED FIRST.

Chapter 3
Cat Senses

Taste and Smell

HORNY PROJECTIONS ON A CAT'S TONGUE HELP IT LAP FLUIDS AND RASP FLESH FROM BONES.

Covering a cat's tongue are horny projections called filiform papillae. These not only make an efficient cleaning mechanism, but are ideal for lapping up fluids and for rasping flesh from bones. The only problem with these filiform papillae is that they slope backwards, towards the throat, making it difficult for a cat to avoid swallowing anything that the horny projections have picked up — including the cat's own fur! The tongue is extremely sensitive and is, like the human tongue, able to detect sweet, sour, bitter and salty tastes, as well as identify temperature and texture.

More finely honed, however, is a cat's sense of smell — it has more than three times as many cells which are capable of detecting smells compared to us mere humans! A cat's nose is filled with tiny bony plates called turbinals which effectively increase the surface area to accommodate more 'scent-sensitive' cells. This highly developed sense is used at both short range to detect food and, at long range, to sniff out potential sexual partners. Cats have scent glands on their chins and temples and spread their scent by rubbing their heads and bodies against objects — table and chair legs, door frames, their

owner's legs, and even shopping bags in which their food is carried home! Cats of both sexes will also spread their scent and mark their territory by spraying urine.

If you ever see your cat sniffing the air by an open window or door, often it will have an odd looking expression on its face, as if it's smelling something most unpleasant! What is happening is a response called flehmen. This is when a cat seems to open its mouth and curl up its lips. It does this to draw air and any scents into the mouth and across an unusual olfactory organ called Jacobson's organ located on the roof of the mouth. This organ supplements the sensory cells in the nose. Just behind the cat's incisor teeth are two tiny ducts which lead to the Jacobson's organ.

CATS USE THEIR SENSE OF SMELL TO INSPECT POTENTIAL FOOD AND TO SNIFF OUT MATES.

CATS HAVE THREE TIMES AS MANY CELLS CAPABLE OF DETECTING SCENT AS US MERE HUMANS!

Cats' Eyes

In most mammals, smell is the most important sense in locating food and it also acts as an early-warning system in case of danger. In cats, as with man and monkeys, vision is more important. Despite having very large eyes for the size of their heads, cats cannot see in total darkness. They do, however, have extremely good vision in poor light conditions, being able to see up to six times better than human beings. Large flat cells in the back of the eye form a mirror-like structure called the tapetum lucidum, which reflects light that has not been absorbed in passing through the eye and intensifies the information reaching the retina. This light-reflecting structure is what causes cats' eyes to glow in the dark!

Cats are also able to see through an angle of 205 degrees – they have about 120 degrees of binocular vision and a further 80 degrees of monocular vision – and their eyes are able to adapt to different light intensities. They open the iris to its fullest circle to allow in the greatest amount of light possible in very dim conditions, or narrow the iris to a mere slit – often called 'one o'clock eyes' – when the light is stronger. Cats also have a 'third eyelid' or, more correctly, a nictitating membrane. This

BY OPENING AND CLOSING THE IRIS CATS' EYES ADJUST TO DIFFERING LIGHT.

rises from the inside corner of the eye and acts as a further filter to protect the eye in very strong light.

Once it was thought that cats' vision was limited to monochrome, but now it is generally believed they do see in colour, although their sensitivity to colour is less than a quarter of that in humans. It also seems that despite their superb vision, cats are not very good at picking out stationary objects, but are very good at noticing movement and can judge distances very accurately. Most cat owners would agree with this as they've all had experience of their cats sitting and ignoring their new, but immobile, cat toy – until, that is, the new toy is attached

READY TO POUNCE: A STATIONARY TOY IS OF LITTLE INTEREST, BUT A MOVING TARGET IS MORE FUN.

to a piece of string and dragged across the floor, and then kitty turns into tiger! The same thing happens with fingers or toes under a blanket – they'll be right under their noses but ignored completely until wiggled and, no matter how fast you think you are, you'll never be able to beat a cat!

Modern breeders have been able to produce a startling range of eye colours in cats from bright blue to bright, fiery orange. Kittens are born with blue eyes, but they change colour as they grow, turning coppery-brown, orange, yellow or green. Wild cats have copper-coloured or hazel

eyes, which can tend towards yellow or green as the cats age. Wild cats' eyes are also oval in shape and slightly slanted, and breeds that are considered to be closer to the 'natural' or 'wild' cat, such as the Maine Coon, share this eye shape. Selective breeding programmes have altered the 'natural' eye shape so now cats eyes may be rounder or more slanted.

Contrary to popular belief, the colour of cats' eyes is not determined by the colour of their coats, although some breed standards do link the two. For example, silver tabbies are often required by show

ODD-EYED WHITE CATS ARE OFTEN
DEAF IN ONE, OR BOTH, EARS.

standards to have green eyes but, genetically, they can also have copper- or gold-coloured eyes. The only eye colour that is linked to coat colour is blue: blue eyes are caused by forms of albinism that lead to a lack of pigmentation in both the cat's coat and in the iris of the eye. This is especially common in cats with a high proportion of white in their coats.

Unfortunately, white coated, blue-eyed cats are likely to be deaf because the gene that causes the lack of pigment also causes fluid in the organ of Corti (the hearing receptor in the cochlea) to dry up. The original Turkish Angoras were usually white cats and often had odd eyes — one blue and one orange — and were also usually deaf in one or both ears.

BLUE EYES ARE THE ONLY EYE COLOUR LINKED
TO COAT COLOUR. THIS COLOURING IS CAUSED
BY FORMS OF ALBINISM THAT LEAD TO A LACK
OF PIGMENTATION IN THE COAT AND IRIS.

The Cat's Whiskers

All over a cat's body are sensitive nerves that respond not only to direct pressure, such as the stroke of a human hand or the licking tongue of a mother cat, but to subtle changes in air pressure.

The most noticeable 'sensors' are their whiskers, the slightly thicker hairs over their eyes and on their chins, and the hairs on the back of their front paws. These latter 'whiskers' are called vibrissae and it is because they are sensitive to pressure that cats know whether there is enough space for them to crawl through a hole. A cat with damaged whiskers may be able to effect a clean kill in daylight, but it won't be so capable in the dark because its important sensors are impaired.

THIS CAT HAS A MAGNIFICENT SET OF WHISKERS AND VERY VISIBLE VIBRISSAE OVER THE EYES.

THE SENSITIVE NERVES ALL OVER A KITTEN'S BODY RESPOND TO THE PRESSURE OF A MOTHER'S CLEANSING TONGUE.

35

As hunters, cats are highly attuned to sounds beyond the range of human hearing. Cats are able to perceive high frequency sounds up to around 65 kHz (65,000 cycles per second) while we mere mortals have a limit of around 20 kHz (20,000 cycles per second – around the top notes of a violin). For very low notes up to 2 kHz, man and cats are on a par in sensitivity, but as the cycles increase to 4 kHz, when human hearing is at its optimum, cats can still 'out-hear' us! This is partly because the shape of their ears helps to concentrate sound much more effectively than ours and also because cats' ears are more manoeuvrable than ours, allowing them to focus upon the slightest noise and identify its direction.

CATS' HEARING ABILITY IS FAR GREATER THAN THAT OF HUMANS.

Wild animals generally have pricked-up ears – the elephant is a rare exception – and ears that droop are generally an indication that the species has been domesticated for some time. Cats in the wild would be at a great disadvantage if their hearing was in any way impaired and, furthermore, any abnormality that did produce drooping ears would probably be halted through natural selection. Nevertheless, not all cats have pointed ears: for more than two centuries, cats with pendulous 'drop-eared', or 'folded' ears have been recorded. The first (unauthenticated) mention was in a British magazine in 1796 and told of cats in China with what were described as 'hanging ears'. In 1938, zoologists found a second example, which appeared to be a rare mutation that was initially believed to be confined to white, long-haired cats. In 1961, Susie, a white kitten, was born on a farm in Perthshire, Scotland, with ears that folded flat on its head. The unique ears are due to a dominant gene that causes varying degrees of 'fold'.

THE EARS OF THE SCOTTISH FOLD ARE FOLDED FLAT AGAINST ITS HEAD.

Susie had what is now called a 'single fold', where her ears bent forwards. Controlled breeding oversaw the early development of the breed to first produce a variety of short-haired cats now called Scottish Fold. Today's show cats have 'triple folds', so their ears are set flat against the head, as though they are wearing a little cap! Susie also carried a gene for long hair, which could also be carried by short-haired offspring, so both long-haired and short-haired Scottish Folds, although rare, are recognised breeds in America. In Britain, however, the breed is not recognised because a crippling skeletal problem caused by homozygosity (having a matching pair of genes for folded ears – the result of breeding Fold-to-Fold cats) does not show up in kittens until they are at least four months old. A second breed with a striking mutation is the American Curl, whose ears curl backwards from the face towards the centre of the head.

A GENETIC MUTATION HAS CAUSED THE EARS OF THE AMERICAN CURL TO TURN IN TOWARDS THE CENTRE OF ITS HEAD.

Chapter 4
Feline Forms

The average domestic cat stands about 30 cm (12 in) high at the shoulder and weighs in at about 5 kg (9 lb) – although the gentle giants of the cat world, Maine Coons, can tip the scales at 9 kg (20 lb). There are three basic cat shapes:

Cobby: a solidly built cat with a short, rounded head and short legs

Muscular: a medium build, medium legs and a slightly rounded head

Lithe: light build, long, slim legs and a narrow wedge-shaped head

THE AVERAGE CAT STANDS ABOUT 30 CM (12 IN) AT THE SHOULDER, BUT ITS FLEXIBILITY ALLOWS IT TO STRETCH MUCH FURTHER.

Most cat breeds are not defined by coat colour or the patterns of the coats because many breeds share the same attributes. Instead, cat breeds are more often differentiated by the shapes of their bodies and faces, and sometimes, by any distinctive physical features such as the Scottish Fold's ears, or the Manx cat's lack of a tail.

The differences in form, from the compact cobby to the sinuous, lithe body of Oriental breeds, in fact follow a geographical pattern from west to east. The heavier, and more compact cobby cats with their solid bodies, broad chests, strong legs, rounded paws and thick tails, evolved essentially through natural selection in cold climates. In short, they were 'built' to retain as much body heat as possible. Modern shorthair examples are the British Shorthair and American Shorthair, the Manx and the Chartreux. The original long-haired cats, known as 'Longhairs' in the UK and 'Persians' in the

MANX

BURMESE

NORWEGIAN FOREST CAT

PERSIAN

US, are also thickset and muscular allowing them to endure the cold winters in the high mountains of Turkey, Iran and the Caucasus. Other cat breeds, such as the Norwegian Forest and Siberian Forest cats and the American Maine Coon, evolved in cold climates from farm cats that spent much of their lives outdoors.

At the other end of the body-type scale, the lithe bodies of the Oriental breeds evolved in warm climates, where losing excess body heat is more important than retaining it. Oriental breeds, such as the Siamese, Burmese and Tonkinese, are generally marked by their large ears, long legs, slender bodies and thin tails.

The lean, muscular cats are often called 'semi-foreign' as they fall some way between the chunky, cold-weather cats of the cobby type and the lithe Oriental cats from the warmer climates of Africa and Asia. In breeds such as the Turkish Angora, the Russian Blue and the Abyssinian, the slender but muscular legs, oval paws and long, tapering tails characteristic of the Oriental breeds can be seen.

AMERICAN SHORTHAIR

ORIENTAL

ABYSSINIAN

41

Fur Types and Coat Lengths

Domestic cats divide roughly into two main types: long-haired cats and short-haired cats. In the wild, a cat's coat would evolve to suit its life and habitat. It's likely that the original cats had short hair, which is much easier to groom and maintain – although there are modern long-haired wild cats whose coats are longer to protect them in winter months from extremely low temperatures in northern climates. While modern short-haired and long-haired cats, such as Persians, have been bred for their appearances, colours and coat lengths, if all pedigree cats were left to breed freely, within just a few generations, the offspring would revert to being wild cats!

Three different types of hair go to make up a cat's fur. The first type of hair is called down, which is the soft hair making the base coat. The second hair type, which makes the middle layer of fur, is called awn, while the longest hairs are called guard hairs.

Not all cats have all three types of hair. There is evidence that the Aztecs had 'hairless' cats and, for a short time in the 1880s, a breed called the Mexican Hairless cat was popular. The modern breed of cats called the Sphynx is not completely hairless, but covered in soft down hairs.

BRITISH SHORTHAIR

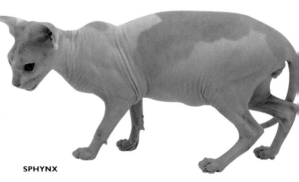

LONG-HAIRED BLUE AND CREAM

SPHYNX

AMERICAN WIREHAIR

DEVON REX

While the Devon Rex has all three types of hairs, they are severely distorted, creating a curly coat. In other 'Rexed', or 'curly-coated' cats, such as the Cornish Rex and the American Wirehair, the guard hairs are absent and so the fur is luxuriously soft and curled. The Angora, one of the oldest breeds of cat from ancient Turkey, has no woolly undercoat, making for a fine and silky coat, while the Longhair (Persian) has the deepest down and the longest guard hairs – up to 12.5 cm (5 in) long.

PERSIAN

ANGORA

Coat markings and patterns

In spite of the wonderful array of different colours and patterns in modern cat breeds, underneath all that luxuriant fur, all cats are basically tabbies! Since the ancestor of the modern domesticated cat was African Wild Cat, all cats do inherit some form of the tabby gene. Like their hunting instinct, the tabby gene is a legacy of the cat's origins and a reminder that all cats can return at any time! The name 'tabby' is thought to come from Attabiya, an area of the city of Baghdad, Iraq, which was once famous for producing a type of watered silk fabric, or taffeta, the pattern of which was similar to that of the cat's coat.

TABBY – EXOTIC SHORTHAIR

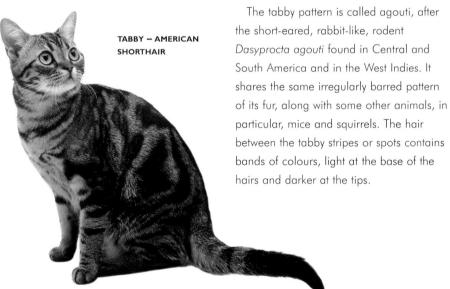

TABBY – AMERICAN SHORTHAIR

The tabby pattern is called agouti, after the short-eared, rabbit-like, rodent *Dasyprocta agouti* found in Central and South America and in the West Indies. It shares the same irregularly barred pattern of its fur, along with some other animals, in particular, mice and squirrels. The hair between the tabby stripes or spots contains bands of colours, light at the base of the hairs and darker at the tips.

SPOTTED TABBY PATTERN – BRITISH SHORTHAIR   **MACKEREL TABBY PATTERN – NORWEGIAN FOREST CAT**

There are four basic types of tabby markings in cats: mackerel (striped), ticked (Abyssinian), classic (blotched) and spotted. While each pattern looks different, they are all mutations of the same naturally dominant tabby gene, the agouti allele. Mackerel tabby stripes run in narrow, parallel lines from the spine down the flanks to the belly. Classic tabbies have wider stripes in swirls on the flanks called 'oysters', which have a blotch in the centre.

TICKED TABBY PATTERN – PIXIEBOB

CLASSIC TABBY PATTERN – MAINE COON

45

Ticked tabbies have a much more subtle patterning with the clearer markings restricted to the head, legs, tail and body. Ticking is where there are different bands of colour on each individual hair and the gene for this was first noted in the Abyssinian. Spotted tabbies, as their name suggests, have spotted bodies, with the pattern formed when the tabby stripes are broken up. While the spots on many American and European breeds follow the lines of mackerel tabbies, other breeds such as the Mau have a random pattern of spots, and the spots on the Ocicat follow the lines of the classic tabby, swirling around the flanks.

EGYPTIAN MAU

While all cats inherit some form of the agouti allele, with selective breeding it has been possible to create a whole range of coat patterns including self (single, solid colours), spotted, tipped and pointed patterns. In the wild, these new patterns would have reduced the cat's ability to camouflage itself for hunting but, as cats became domestic pets, and no longer relied on hunting to survive, these genetically mutated patterns became prized for their beautiful appearance.

Geneticists call the agouti allele 'dominant', and denote the gene as A. Any cat that inherits gene A from at least one parent will have a patterned coat and is denoted as A-.

OCICAT

Cat Colours

Solid colours exist in cats' coats because there is a genetically recessive gene, an alternative gene to the agouti allele, called 'non-agouti' and denoted as a. Cats that inherit this gene from both parents (denoted as aa) will have a self coat of single, solid, even colour, although on close examination you may find hidden tabby markings. This is called 'ghosting' and can be easily seen in kittens before it fades as they mature.

The first mutation away from the tabby's agouti-banded hair to a single colour was most likely to black, as this colour is seen in other big cats such as leopards and panthers. Other mutations occurred for red and white along with dilutions of solid colours, and these few genetic variations created the basic framework for the many beautiful coat colours that exist in modern cat breeds.

All coloured hair contains melanin, a

SOLID COLOUR — BRITISH SHORTHAIR

pigment in the body of humans and certain animals, that occurs in the skin and in the hair. Melanin is made up of two components: eumelanin, which produces black and brown pigment granules, and phaeomelanin, which produces red and yellow pigment granules. The colour of cats' hair is dependent on whether or not

47

RED CAT

theses pigment granules are present in the shafts of each hair. The pigment granules are made in skin cells called melanocytes, and where and in what pattern these cells are distributed on the cat's body is genetically determined. Historically, certain patterns and colours have been more prevalent in some countries than in others. This is due to the long-term genetic influence of early members of the cat population on later generations. This influence is called the 'founder effect'.

BLACK PERSIAN

Feline Genetics

The basis of inherited characteristics is in cats' genes: every cell (at some stage) has a nucleus. Each nucleus contains 38 chromosomes arranged into 19 pairs. Each chromosome is made up of a double helix of DNA (deoxyribonucleic acid), which in turn is made up of thousands of genes. Each gene is made up of four proteins denoted as A, T, C and G, and when these genes are combined, all the information needed to 'make a cat' is provided.

Every time a cell dies, a new cell is made and its chromosomes are copied. RNA (ribonucleic acid) is generated to match both strands of the double helix and this is then used to provide a template so that new DNA can be formed. Normally this copying is perfect – like a photocopier churning out sheet after sheet of copies of the original information. Every so often, however – just like a photocopier

THE SNOWSHOE IS THE RESULT OF A SIAMESE/AMERICAN SHORTHAIR CROSS.

getting jammed or two pieces of paper getting fed through at the same time – a genetic 'mistake' or mutation in one gene gets passed along. In genetics – unlike the average photocopier – the rate of 'mistakes' that get passed on is one gene in one million copies!

In genetics, information contained in the genes is passed along the generations. Egg and sperm cells contain only 19 chromosomes each. At conception the 19 chromosomes of the egg cell join up to the 19 chromosomes of the sperm cell, creating a new set of 19 pairs. So a kitten inherits half its characteristics from its mother, and the other half from its father.

A KITTEN INHERITS HALF ITS CHARACTERISTICS FROM EACH PARENT.

Specific information, such as that for particular colouring or markings, are always in the same site on each of the chromosomes. In a pair of chromosomes, this pair of sites is called the 'allele'. If both chromosomes contain the same information, the instructions are homozygous. If the instructions in the two chromosomes at the allele site contain different information, the instructions are heterozygous.

Genetic variations in characteristics, such as coat length, pattern or colour are described as dominant when only one copy of chromosome information (one half of the pair of chromosomes) is needed to show the variation. If two copies are needed (from both chromosomes in the pair) for a variation to become evident, this is described as recessive. The original feline traits, such as the agouti allele (the gene for which is called *A*) of the tabby cat, and the original trait of shorthair (the gene for which is called *L*) tend to be dominant. When the mutations occurred, the recessive genes were produced, giving rise to new variations such as the non-agouti gene *a* for the self- or single-coloured cat, and the recessive gene for long hair (denoted as *l*).

TONKINESE SHORTHAIR

Nevertheless, a cat that displays the dominant trait – tabby markings or short hair for example – may itself also be the carrier of a recessive trait – for a self colour or long hair – hidden away in its genes! A cat with a recessive trait must be homozygous, with no 'alternative' genes. But two heterozygous short-haired cats, both having *Ll* alleles (the dominant *L* for short hair and the recessive *l* for long hair), will have an average of two *Ll* kittens (one dominant and one recessive gene; result: short hair), one *LL* kitten (with both the dominant trait genes; result: short hair), and one kitten with long hair, carrying both recessive (*ll*) genes. Because three of the kittens have short hair, their physical

50

PERSIAN

appearance gives no clue as to which carries the recessive *l* gene that would enable them to produce long-haired kittens.

As well as the dominant agouti (*A*) gene for the tabby and the dominant *L* gene for short hair, the dominant feline traits are *B* (black), *C* (full colour or solid), *D* (dense, dark colour), *I* (inhibitor or 'silvering'), *S* (white spotting or bicoloured), *T* (striped or mackerel tabby), T^a (Abyssinian or ticked tabby), *W* (white, masking all other colours) and *O* (orange or sex-linked red).

BLUE BRITISH SHORTHAIR

Cats with densely coloured self coats, in black, chocolate brown, cinnamon and sex-linked red, must have at least one copy of the *D* (dense) gene which is dominant and makes for hairs that are packed with pigment to give a rich, deep colour. Other cats, with 'dilute' coats, in blues, lilacs, fawns and sex-linked cream, have two copies of the recessive dilute (*d*) gene which gives fewer pigment granules in each hair and creates paler colour effects. It is also believed that there is a further' modifying' dilute gene, called D^m. This is more dominant than the *d* gene, but can interact with it. So if a cat carries both the *dd* dilute trait and the D^m gene, there will be a further modification to the colour: blue!

DILUTE – PERSIAN CALICO

RED ABYSSINIAN

WHITE ORIENTAL

Sex-linked Red: Ginger Toms and Calico Queens

The gene for red or orange in cats is believed to be located at a specific site on the sex-determining chromosome, the X chromosome. In its dominant form the gene O for sex-linked red will make the cat red haired. In its recessive form o, the gene will allow whatever other colour the cat is carrying to show through.

A tomcat with an XY chromosome combination – one Y male and one female X chromosome – can only have one copy of the gene. If he carries O, the dominant gene for sex-linked red, he will be ginger. If he carries one o, however, he can be any other colour. The queen, because she has the XX chromosome combination – two female X chromosomes – has two copies. If she carries two copies of O, she will be red. But if she carries two o recessive genes, she will be another colour. It is the oo combination of genes that will make her

a tortoiseshell – or calico, as they are known in the US – and this patterning, called mosaicking, is the result of the interaction of all the other colour-controlling genes, so it is possible to have 'torties' in both solid and dilute colours.

Dominant over all the other colour genes is the gene for white (W). This can mean an all-over white colour or, with the S gene, white spotting. Bicoloured or tri-coloured cats are white coated with patches of other colours. There are two types of bicolouring: the standard bicolour is defined as a one-third to half-white coloured cat, but with the white confined to the legs and 'underpants', while the second type, the Van pattern – originally associated with the Turkish Van cat but now seen in others – consists of predominantly white with solid or tortie patches on the head and tail only.

The Western breeds of cats – the British, American and European Shorthairs, Maine Coons and Norwegian Forest Cats – all began with traditional colours: black and

TURKISH VAN   BI-COLOUR BRITISH SHORTHAIR CREAM AND WHITE

dilute blue, red and dilute cream, solid white and bicoloured versions. In Eastern countries, however, the original colours were chocolate and dilute lilac, cinnamon and dilute fawn. Today, with modern breeds, coat colours have been transposed from west to east, from east to west and from one breed to another. So, it is now possible to have British Shorthairs in 'eastern' colours and eastern cats like the Burmese, with 'western' colours such as red and cream!

Although there are only a few genes responsible for other solid colours,

depending on the cat, breeders and breed associations often give the same 'genetic' colour a different name. Lilac is also known as lavender; black Oriental Shorthairs are also called ebony; while genetically chocolate-brown-coloured Oriental Shorthairs are called 'Havana' in Britain and 'Chestnut' in North America. Genetically red and white Turkish Van cats are called 'Auburn and White', while tortie-and-white cats are called Calicos by the CFA (see page19) because their colouring resembles printed calico fabric.

CREAM BURMESE – AN ORIENTAL CAT WITH 'WESTERN' COLOUR.

Chapter 5
The Breed Directory

Long-haired Breeds

In the wild, there are no long-haired cats, although some, like lions, do grow ruffs or manes of longer fur. Even the Amur Tiger and the Snow Leopard, which both endure particularly harsh winters near the snow line, only grow hairs about 12.5 cm (5 in) long, which size for size, are quite short compared to domesticated long-haired cats. Long hair on a wild cat would be impractical: it would get tangled and matted, pick up burrs and thorns, as well as parasites and be impossible to groom properly.

IN THE WILD A LION MAY GROW A LONGER 'RUFF' OR MANE AROUND THE NECK.

THE MAINE COON'S LONG COAT IS WATER-REPELLENT; A CHARACTERISTIC THAT DEVELOPED OVER TIME TO SUIT ITS HARSH NATURAL ENVIRONMENT.

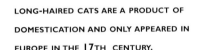

LONG-HAIRED CATS ARE A PRODUCT OF DOMESTICATION AND ONLY APPEARED IN EUROPE IN THE 17TH CENTURY.

Long-haired cats are only mentioned in historical records long after the cat had become domesticated, and were only mentioned in Europe in the 17th century when it was claimed that a long-haired cat was imported into Italy from Persia in 1620 by Pietro de Valle. At the end of the century, French scientist and traveller, Nicholas Fabri de Peiresc, brought a long-haired cat to France from Turkey, and the first clearly described long-haired cats in Europe were given the name Angora cats, called after the capital city of Turkey – now Ankara – where these cats appear to have been known for centuries.

By the time of the cat shows of the 19th century, both Persian cats, said to have come from the Persian province of Chorazan, and the Angora were known in Europe, and considered as 'status symbol' pets. But the Persian type became the most fancied and the Angora was soon to disappear from show benches and homes. Recently, the original Turkish Angora Cat became established as a new breed in the United States from imported cats bred deliberately at Ankara Zoo to protect the species from extinction.

TURKISH ANGORA

For most people, the name 'Persian' thus became synonymous with long-haired cats, although the British Cat Fancy (CFA) now officially uses the designation Long-haired for self-coloured cats, with other colours classified as separate breeds. In the United States, these cats are still called Persians, and the different colours are listed as varieties.

After the Crystal Palace Cat Show in 1871, in London, standards for Persians and Angoras were written by Harrison Weir. Subsequent breeding within the guidelines has meant that stocky build remains an essential characteristic of Longhairs, but their faces are much shorter and their coats much longer.

There are, however, some long-haired cats which are not Persian and hail from climates where a longer, thicker coat is an asset. The Norwegian Forest Cat and the Maine Coon have a different body type to Longhair/Persian cats, with slimmer legs and trunks and narrower faces with longer noses. Despite their long hair, these cats don't require as much grooming as their 'exotic' cousins whose fur sheds copiously at each stroke of their silky coats!

NORWEGIAN FOREST CAT

Angora/Oriental Longhair

Date of origin: **1970s**

Place of origin: **Britain**

Ancestry: **Siamese/Abyssinian crosses**

Other names: **Javanese (Europe), Mandarin and previously known in the US as Oriental Longhair**

Colours:

Self (solid) colours: **black, chocolate, cinnamon, red, blue, lilac, fawn, cream, caramel, apricot and white (blue-, green- and odd-eyed)**

Tortoiseshell colours: **tortoiseshell, chocolate tortoiseshell, cinnamon, blue, lilac, fawn and caramel tortoiseshell**

Smoke, Shaded, Silver Shaded and Tipped colours: **as for self and tortie except white**

Tabbies (all patterns): **brown, chocolate, cinnamon, red, blue, lilac, fawn, cream, caramel, tortie, chocolate tortie, cinnamon tortie, blue tortie, lilac tortie, fawn tortie and caramel tortie**

Silver Tabby colours (all patterns): **as for standard tabbies**

Coat length: **medium-long**

Type of fur: **very fine with tendency to curl, no thick undercoat**

Size: **2.5–5.5 kg (5–11 lb)**

BLACK ANGORA/ORIENTAL LONGHAIR

The Angora breed suffers from a little confusion because it has a number of names: in continental Europe it is known as the Javanese – even though some North American cat associations use this name to refer to some colours of the Balinese! In North America, the British Angora was once called the Oriental Longhair, implying that it was a descendent of the Oriental Shorthair. There is now, however, a true breed called the Oriental Longhair (see page 107) with that descent.

The most important thing to note about the Angora, is that this cat is not related to either the Oriental Longhairs, or the Turkish Angora saved from extinction by the breeding programme at Ankara Zoo and now a protected breed. The modern Angora, would perhaps best be called the 'British Angora' since this breed was developed in the UK by Maureen Silson in the mid 1960s when a sorrel (red) Abyssinian was mated with a Seal Point Siamese in an effort to produce a Siamese

BLACK SILVER SHADED ANGORA/ORIENTAL LONGHAIR

61

with ticked points! The descendants inherited the cinnamon trait – producing cinnamon Oriental Shorthairs – and the gene for long hair, which led to the creation of the first Angora, who was called Cuckoo.

The elegant, lithe-bodied Angora, is one of the oldest breeds of cat. It may well have been the first long-haired cat to arrive in Europe, although it was never as popular as the more sturdily built Persian. The Angora has a similar temperament to the other Oriental breeds, being lively and inquisitive, but also capable of long periods of inactivity, which they love to spend sleeping in warm, comfortable places.

Angoras have a very fine, silky coat and, having no woolly undercoat, they require less grooming than Persians/Longhairs and their coat lies flat on their bodies. Angora coats are slow to mature and young cats often have short coats for quite some time. Their bodies are carried on long, slim and well-muscled legs – the forelegs are shorter than the hind legs – and end in small, oval paws with tufts of fur at the toes. Their tails, which are carried up, are long and fluffy and taper to a fine end. Their ears are large and pricked atop a small (in proportion to the body) wedge-shaped head with large, almond shaped eyes. Angoras' eyes are green in all coat colours – except in white cats, when they are blue- or odd-eyed.

BLACK ANGORA

Turkish Angora

It has been suggested that the Turkish Angora traces its descent from the manul, or Pallas' cat (*Felis manul*) found in the steppes, rocky terrain and wooded mountainsides of central Asia. This handsome wild cat is orangey-grey with black and white head markings, and the story goes that the Tartars domesticated it and took it to Turkey. It is more likely though, that the Turkish Angora is a distant relative of the Persian, with the two lines developing separately over the centuries and the Turkish Angora becoming established in the Turkish capital, Angora (now Ankara). It seems that the gene for

Date of origin: 1400s
Place of origin: Turkey
Ancestry: unknown, possibly household cats
Other names: none
Colours:
Self (solid) and Tortie colours: white, black, red, blue, cream, tortie and blue–cream
Smoke and Shaded colours: as for self and tortie except white
Tabby colours (Classic and Mackerel): brown, red, blue and cream
Silver Tabby colours (Classic Mackerel): silver
Bicolours: all self and tortie colours, with white
Coat length: medium–long
Type of fur: fine and silky with negligible undercoat
Size: 2.5–5 kg (6–11 lb)

WHITE TURKISH ANGORA

long hair mutated in – or spread to – a group of cats with the lithe body build (known to breeders as 'foreign'), and because there were limited opportunities for breeding outside the group, the long-coated characteristic became fixed, so that a true-breeding, long-haired cat with a foreign body evolved.

In the 16th century, Turkish Angoras were sent as diplomatic gifts by the Sultan to Europe and were the first long-haired cats to be seen there. At first they were very popular, but later they lost ground to the Persians and newer Longhair breeds. While they continued to thrive in their homeland, by the end of World War II, the Turkish Angora was extinct in the Western world. In the 1950s and 1960s however, breeding

pairs of Turkish Angoras were said to have been brought from Ankara Zoo and taken to the USA where a breeding programme was established, while other Turkish Angoras were taken to Sweden and Britain. These cats formed the foundation stock for the pedigree Turkish Angoras of North America and continental Europe, and the Turkish cats of Britain.

In many respects, the Turkish Angora is similar in appearance to the Angora (see page 60) as both share the elegant, lithe body shape with long, slim legs. Furthermore, both have small paws with tufts of fur on the toes and small wedge-shaped heads. The ears are large and pricked and, like the Angora, the Turkish has a long, fluffy tail, carried elegantly up.

The medium-long coat is very fine and silky, and shimmers when the cat moves. It is shed in the summer months, when the Turkish Angora appears more of a short-hair cat – with the exception of its luxurious tail.

In Turkey, Angoras were to be seen in many colours, each with their own descriptive names such as sarman (red tabby) and teku (silver tabby). Today, Turkish Angoras are recognised in a variety of colours, shades and patterns, such as tortie-and-white, black – which must be coal black and solid from the roots to the tip of each hair – and Smoke. Smoke Turkish Angoras appear to be full-coloured cats when they are in repose, but when the cat moves, the subtle colours of the undercoat become apparent. Combined with their inherent grace, the colourings of the winter coat do indeed look like swirls of smoke.

It is, however, the blue-eyed, white Turkish Angoras – which regrettably like other white cats of most other breeds are often deaf in either one or both ears – who are the great favourites. To many fanciers though, the Ankara kedi, as they are known still in Turkey, the 'odd–eyed white' – one blue and one orange – is the classic colour and eye combination of the historical, pure breed.

Balinese

Date of origin: **1950s**

Place of origin: **USA**

Ancestry: **Long-haired Siamese**

Other names: **sometimes called Javanese in the US**

Colours:

CFA recognised: **lilac point, blue point, chocolate point and seal point**

Other colours/variants: **Javanese point colours in CFA – seal point, seal tortie tabby point, chocolate tortie point, red tabby point, blue tabby point, seal tabby point and chocolate tabby point**

Coat length: **medium–long, with a tendency to curl, but generally shorter than other long-haired breeds**

Type of fur: **fine and silky with no undercoat**

Size: **2.5–5 kg (6–11 lb)**

For many years, long-haired kittens had appeared from time to time in the litters of particular Siamese bloodlines. In 1928, a long-haired Siamese was registered in Britain with the CFA, but generally, such long-haired offspring were regarded by cat breeders and fanciers as 'faulty' since their long hair disqualified them from being shown as Siamese. In the main, these lovely cats were passed on to owners as house pets. In the 1940s, however, Marion Dorsey produced Balinese kittens and a number of breeders in the US began working towards gaining recognition for these cats as a separate breed. Since the gene for long hair (*l*) (see pages 49–53) is inherited in a recessive manner, any long-haired Siamese must be homozygous (true breeding) for long hair. This means that it must carry two of the longhair genes, and that any offspring that result from mating two such cats will also be long haired.

In 1955, 'Longhaired Siamese' were exhibited, but breeders of Siamese cats protested at the name. The breed was renamed Balinese, a name suggested by these cats' svelte lines and graceful movements, emphasised by the flow of their long, silky coat. Indeed, the Balinese in motion is reminiscent of the dancers of the

Indonesian island, even though they hail from North America!

The Balinese resembles the Siamese in most ways: it has a slender, fine-boned, sleek body with a long, wedge-shaped head and deep blue, almond-shaped eyes. From the front, a Balinese's head is wide between the ears (which may be tufted), narrowing to a fine muzzle in a straight line, while in profile the nose should be straight and the chin strong. From all aspects the Balinese is a splendidly elegant-looking cat. The coat is medium long, without the fluffy undercoat of other Longhair cats, and the hairs lie more or less flat against the body. This also makes these cats easier to groom and keep tangle-free than other long-haired cats.

CREAM POINT BALINESE

67

From a distance it can be easy to mistake a Balinese for a Siamese – that is until you see the Balinese's tail. Long and plumed, and like the Siamese, no kink or squint is allowed. In colouring, as with other long-haired, pointed cats, there is less contrast between body and point colour than is normally seen in Siamese. The CFA in America recognises only four basic point colours: seal, blue, chocolate and lilac.

SEAL TORTOISESHELL BALINESE

Breeders in other associations in Britain and Australia have, in addition, produced red-, cream-, tortie- and tabby-point Balinese, which are recognised by the CFA under the breed name of Javanese (see note right). As with all pointed cats, the coats of the Balinese darken with age, making a show cat's career quite short.

As might be expected, Balinese share many characteristics as pets with Siamese. They are incredibly acrobatic – their tubular bodies allow them to perform the greatest feats in tight spaces (mainly kitchen drawers and cupboards!). They love climbing – especially up curtains – and playing in shopping bags and will often ride on the shoulders of their owners. Highly affectionate, they also demand attention in return, and yet they still manage to retain an elegant air of aloofness! Lively and spirited cats though they are, the Balinese are almost, though not quite, as talkative as Siamese!

Note:

In North America, the name Javanese is used to describe the varieties of Balinese cats that do not correspond to the four traditional Siamese point colours. In New Zealand, the self and spotted varieties of Balinese are called Javanese, while in Britain, the Javanese is a separate breed – the result of attempts to recreate the Angora. The Javanese was granted Championship status in 1984, and has recently been introduced to the USA.

Birman

Date of origin: unknown

Place of origin: Burma (now Myanmar) or France

Ancestry: disputed

Other names: Sacred Cat of Burma

Colours:

Self (solid) and Tortie Points: seal, chocolate, red, blue, lilac, cream, seal tortie, blue tortie, lilac tortie and chocolate tortie

Tabby Points: colours as for self and tortie points

Coat length: long, with full ruff around neck and slightly curled on stomach

Type of fur: fine and silky, snarl- and tangle-resistant

Size: 4.5–8 kg (10–18 lb)

A cat of mystery, the Birman is also known as the Sacred Cat of Burma, although it has no connection with the Burmese breed (see page 170). With its pale-coloured body, dark points (mask, ears, tails and legs) and long coat, the Birman does bear a resemblance to the Colourpoint Longhair (Himalayan Persian in US) (see page 79 except for one striking feature – the white gloves on the Birman's paws, which are possibly due to a recessive white-spotting gene, although the romantic tale of the Birman's origins is far more entertaining.

SEAL TABBY POINT BIRMAN

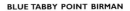

BLUE TABBY POINT BIRMAN

The legend goes that before the time of Buddha, the Khmer people of Southeast Asia built beautiful temples to honour their gods, in particular, the god Song-Hyo and the goddess Tsun-Kyan-Kse. A golden figure of the goddess, with sapphire eyes, was kept at the temple of Lao-Tsun, guarded by 100 pure-white cats. One of these cats was called Sinh, the companion of an old priest called Mun-Ha — whose silver-white beard was said to have been braided by the god Song-Hyo himself. One night, foreign raiders attacked the temple, killing Mun-Ha as he knelt in devotion before the statue of the goddess. Immediately, Sinh jumped on the body of his master and faced the goddess. The soul of the priest entered the cat and, as it did so, its eyes became sapphire-blue, like those of the goddess. The cat's face, ears and legs took on the colour of the fertile land — except for the paws, which remained pure white because, according to the legend, they had touched the priest's beard. (On the Birman's rear paws, the white 'boots' extend up the back of the hock to a point known in North America as the 'laces'.)

BLUE POINT BIRMAN

The transformation amazed the other priests, giving them the courage to drive off the raiders. Seven days later, Sinh died, carrying with it into paradise, the soul of the priest Mun-Ha. But the next morning, all the other white temple cats had also been transformed and, from then on, the sacred golden cats were protected by the priests, who believed they had custody of the souls of their dead brethren.

In the 1920s, French breeders introduced the Birman to Europe. The original Birmans of France were said to have been a gift from the priests of a new temple of Lao-Tsun in the mountains of Tibet. Two cats were reputedly sent to France, with one cat – the male – dying en route. The female cat was pregnant, however, and became the founder of the Birman breed in Europe. A less romantic version of the Birman's origin is that they were a breed

CHOCOLATE POINT BIRMAN

CHOCOLATE BIRMAN

RED TABBY BIRMAN

SEAL POINT BIRMAN

produced in France by matings between Siamese and long-haired black and white cats. Whatever its origins, the Birman is a beautiful cat that became well established in France, until the feline population was decimated during World War II. After the war, the breed was reduced to just two individuals, and it was some time before the breed could recover fully. The Birman was introduced to England in 1966 and to the USA in 1967.

73

BLUE POINT BIRMAN

A strong cat, with a stocky body, thickset legs and large, round paws, the Birman is a very gentle and highly intelligent cat. Its coat is not as fluffy in texture as the Himalayan/Colourpoint Longhair, but more silky – like that of a Turkish Angora in length and texture. In winter months, a ruff around the neck is apparent. For many fanciers, the Birman's most striking features are the eyes that are almost round, slightly slanted and a beautiful, deep sapphire-blue.

LILAC POINT BIRMAN

The Seal Point and the Blue Point Birman were the original colours of the breed introduced by the French in the 1920s, and for some purists these remain the only true Birman colours, although breeders have introduced other point colourings including chocolate and lilac (where the points are a pinkish-grey, with the nose leather to match), red (flame), tortoiseshell and tabby points, which must show clear 'frown' marks between the eyes and lighter 'spectacles', as well as spotted cheek pads, striped legs and a ringed tail. Furthermore, in the US, some breeders have produced short-haired Birman-patterned cats known as Snowshoe Cats or Silver Laces (see page 152).

SEAL TORTOISESHELL BIRMAN

RED BIRMAN

Turkish Van

Date of origin: pre-18th century

Place of origin: Lake Van region, Turkey

Ancestry: household cats

Other names: The Swimming Cat

Colours: the coat is white with markings in the recognised colours on the face and tail

Bicolours: auburn, cream and white with amber, blue or odd eyes

Other colours: black, blue, tortoiseshell, blue-cream, with white

Coat length: long (coat is longer in winter months than in summer)

Type of fur: fine and silky, no undercoat

Size: 3–8.5 kg (7–19 lb)

Unique among small cats, the Turkish Van loves water and is an enthusiastic swimmer! Of the big cats only tigers are strong swimmers, and most domestic cats will shy away from water of any kind – even though they will sit mesmerised for hours watching goldfish in a bowl!

This breed of cat has been domesticated for several hundred years around the area of Lake Van in Turkey. Like the Turkish Angora, the Turkish Van had limited

WHITE-AUBURN TURKISH VAN

opportunities to breed outside of its native region, allowing the long-haired characteristic to become fixed, so that they became a true long-haired breed with a foreign body. Legend has it that the (ideal) white blaze or patch in the centre of the Van's forehead is the thumbprint of Allah and it is also maintained that the cats living locally at the town of Van itself are all-white with odd eyes – one green, one blue. Whatever truth there is in these popular beliefs, the restricted colour of the Van's coat makes it so distinctive that the name is also given to the pattern when it occurs in other breeds.

The modern history of the Turkish Van began in 1955, when two cats were brought home as holiday souvenirs by two British tourists who then went on to establish the breed in the UK. Although the breed spread quickly across Europe, it was not accepted by the registries until 1969. By 1982, Turkish Vans had reached North America where they were accepted by the CFA and TICA.

In the GCCF, however, only the auburn and cream colours are allowed, while the other registries permit black-based colours. While other breeds know the colour simply as red, Turkish Van breeders use a much more poetic designation, 'Auburn', where ideally, the coat should be chalk-white and the red marking confined to the top of the head (markings should not extend below the level of the eyes or beyond the base of the ears) and the full brush of the feathery tail – which is as long as the cat's body. The Auburn pattern, accompanied by large, oval, amber-coloured eyes with pink rims, was the original appearance of the Turkish Van when it arrived in the West in the 1950s.

Tortie-and-White Vans appeared when black was introduced into the breed, but this pattern is difficult to breed to the breed standards – often patches of colour appear on the Van's body – which means that 'perfect' show tortie Vans are scarce, although there are lots of tortie Vans as adored pets!

In their native Turkey, Vans developed an immensely thick winter coat to protect themselves from the freezing temperatures. In the summer, they moult copiously, shedding nearly all the winter coat. The soft coat is water resistant and tends to 'break' open over any curves, rearranging itself with the cat's every move. It is a strongly muscled cat, ideally proportioned for swimming: the body is long, the legs medium length and the paws are rounded and small, with furry toe tufts and pink pads. In temperament the Van retains its sense of independence, inherited from its ancestors – rural cats used to extremes of temperature and tough lives.

Colourpoint Longhair/Himalayan

Date of origin: **1950s**
Place of origin: **UK and USA**
Ancestry: **Longhair, Siamese**
Other names: **Himalayan Persian (USA)**
Colours: **body is ivory/cream with all point colours available**
Coat length: **long (12 cm/5 in)**
Type of fur: **very thick and silky with no woolliness**
Size: **3.5–7 kg (8–15 lb)**

CHOCOLATE COLOURPOINT

RED COLOURPOINT

The Colourpoint Longhair, known more poetically in the US as the Himalayan Persian, is a man-made breed synthesised initially during breeding experiments to solve genetically related diseases in cats. In the 1920s, Swedish geneticist Dr. Tjebbes crossed Siamese, Persian and Birman cats. Then, in the 1930s, two Harvard Medical School researchers in the US decided that further breeding – this time with cats of known pedigree – was necessary in order to establish the inheritance of certain characteristics. They mated Siamese with smoke, silver tabbies and black Longhair/Persians, but this time as a deliberate attempt to establish a Siamese-patterned cat with a Persian coat and body type.

The first Himalayan/Colourpoint Longhair kitten, called Debutante, was born in 1935. In the meantime, other cat breeders were also experimenting in the US and in Britain to develop this breed of beautiful cats. It was called Himalayan, not because of any geographical links to the mountain range, but because this name is used for the same colour patterns in other fancy-bred small livestock, such as rabbits. In Britain, the breed was accepted – but called Colourpoint Longhair – in 1955.

Breeding pedigree Himalayans in the US began in earnest in the 1950s but, because breeders were cautious about showing, few cat lovers knew much about the breed until 1957 when two Himalayans were shown in

San Diego, California, causing a sensation. Two kittens were presented to the president of the newly founded ACFA in request for breed status. When the governing council saw them, they voted 15 to 1 in favour of recognition, with CFA recognition following in the same year.

LILAC COLOURPOINT

Although it is only one of the many Siamese-patterned, long-haired breeds, the Colourpoint/Himalayan is instantly recognisable by its wide head, small, round tipped ears, short, thick and strong legs, bushy tail, short nose and long, thick and silky coat. Dense points and pale body colour are regarded as ideal by judges, but its long coat prevents the Colourpoint/Himalayan from developing quite the same density of point colour that is found in Siamese cats. This is because the Siamese effect is temperature-dependent. Because the hair on the Himalayan/Colourpoint is longer, it traps more air than the flat-lying short hair of the Siamese, thus weakening the point colour. The mask of the mature Colourpoint/Himalayan will cover the face but should not extend over the rest of the head – although toms have more extensive masks than queens.

During its early history as a breed some associations only recognised certain colours, but today, seal point, blue point, chocolate point, lilac point, flame (or red) point, all colours of tortie point and all colours of tabby point are recognised in this exotic and beautiful breed. In an attempt to produce a solid chocolate Longhair/Himalayan, Colourpoint Longhairs/Himalayans were crossed with Burmese. The resulting offspring were developed into the breed now called Tiffannie (see page 104).

Maine Coon

The gentle giant of the feline world, the Maine Coon is one of the oldest natural breeds of North America and is generally regarded as native to the state of Maine. There are a number of legends surrounding its origins, including the popular story that it originated from matings between semi-wild domestic cats and racoons! While genetically impossible, this tale makes sense of the bushy tail, the most common colouring of dark, racoon-like tabby and the adoption of the name Maine Coon – short for racoon. A second theory regarding their origin is that when the French queen, Marie Antoinette, was planning her escape during the French Revolution, she sent her cats to the United States to be cared for until she could be reunited with them.

SILVER TABBY AND WHITE MAINE COON

Date of origin: **1860s**
Place of origin: **USA**
Ancestry: **farm cats**
Other names: **Maine Cat, Maine Shag**
Colours: **all colours and coat patterns, except chocolate, lilac or Siamese patterns**
Coat length: **medium**
Type of fur: **thick and shaggy double coat**
Size: **4–10 kg (9–22 lb)**

83

Delightful as these stories are, it is more likely that the Maine Coon originated in crosses between early Angoras introduced into the US by New England seamen, and short-haired domestic cats. Some Maine Coon fanciers do maintain that the longhair gene was brought to the US by immigrant cats. These, they believe, actually arrived with the Vikings from their trading posts in Greenland and Iceland. A Norse coin from the 11th century was found in Maine, and it is known that cat skins were a valuable trading commodity.

The Maine Coon was well established in the 19th century and had, by this time, evolved into a magnificent, hardy and handsome breed of cat. They were first recorded in literature in 1861 with the

SILVER TABBY CLASSIC MAINE COON

84

mention of a black-and-white known grandly as 'Captain Jenks of the Horse Marines' at Boston and New York cat shows, just when the breed was becoming popular. But when the more flamboyant Persian/Longhair cats arrived on the scene at the end of the 19th century, the Maine Coon declined in popularity as a show cat. However, as terrific mousers on New England farms and as household pets, the Maine Coon continued to reign supreme.

BROWN PATCHED TABBY MAINE COON

BLACK MAINE COON

85

Nevertheless, a small band of dedicated breeders persisted and when pedigree records were established in the 1950s, the Maine Coon once more started to attract attention and interest.

Rugged in coat and build, they withstand the hardest of winters and are also one of the largest breeds physically – males commonly weigh up to 7 kg (15 lb); females up to 5 kg (11 lb) and there are stories of giants of 18 kg (40 lb)! While they enjoy the company of humans, Maine Coons are very

RED SILVER AND WHITE MAINE COON

BLUE/SILVER MAINE COON

TORTOISESHELL TABBY AND WHITE MAINE COON

independent cats – otherwise you'd need a very large lap for them to sit on!

Throughout the history of the Maine Coon there have never been any restrictions – official or otherwise – on the patterns and colours accepted in the breed (with the sole exceptions of lilac, chocolate and Siamese patterns). Consequently Maine Coons are bred in a delightful range of colours including self, bicolours, tortoiseshells, tabby-torties (known as torbies!), shaded and, of course, tabbies – the brown classic tabby is undoubtedly the best known. Originally, only brown tabbies were given the name Maine Coon (because of their close resemblance to racoons) and all other colours and patterns were given the appellation Maine Shags.

WHITE GOLD EYE MAINE COON

87

BROWN TABBY AND WHITE MAINE COON

BLUE TABBY MAINE COON

Eye colours range from green, through gold and copper to blue, with odd eyes in white cats also permitted. In shows, eye and coat colours and combination account for only 15% of the points awarded. Much more important to judges are the head, body and coat condition. The head is ideally slightly longer than it is wide, with high cheekbones and ears that are large, well tufted and wide at the base. The neck is medium long, while the body is long and the chest broad. Unlike a Persian/Longhair, a Maine Coon's legs and tail are long. In spite of its long, thick coat, a Maine Coon is remarkably low maintenance and is water-repellent, so washing is rarely required!

Norwegian Forest Cat

Domestic cats first arrived in Scandinavia some time around AD 1000 via the Vikings' trade routes with the Byzantine Empire in the east, the capital of which was Constantinople (now Istanbul). There is evidence that cats were traded directly between the Vikings and Byzantium, since the cat population of Norway has coat colours in common with Turkish cats that are rare elsewhere in Europe. Long-haired cats are common throughout Scandinavia: while Norway has its 'Wegie', Denmark and Sweden have their own versions called the 'Racekatte' and 'Rugkatt' respectively.

The Norwegian Forest Cat, or Norsk Skaukatt is a uniquely Scandinavian breed of cats, having evolved in the cold, northern climate of Norway. Its exact origins are unknown but, like the Maine Coon, it adapted to living in the cold and wet by growing a magnificent double coat made up of a soft woolly undercoat to keep the body warm and a long, glossy, hanging

Date of origin: 1930s
Place of origin: Norway
Ancestry: farm cats
Other names: Skogkatt or Skaukatt, Wegie
Colours: all coat colours and patterns acceptable, with or without white, except chocolate, lilac and Siamese patterns
Coat length: semi-long
Type of fur: Double. Thick undercoat covered by smooth, water-resistant outer hair
Size: 3–9 kg (7–20 lb)

BROWN TABBY AND WHITE NORWEGIAN FOREST CAT

outer coat designed to shed the snow and rain. As with the Maine Coon, such a coat requires very little grooming, but in common with all other long-haired cats, the outer coat is shed once a year, leaving just the magnificent bushy tail to show that it is truly a long-haired cat. The heavily furred tail – which reaches to the shoulder blades – is long and carried high.

The Wegie's large size, strong legs – the hind legs are longer than the forelegs – large, heavy paws and strong, sharp claws make it a champion climber – perhaps these very agile cats are the descendants of the mythical giant cats that pulled the

BLUE AND WHITE NORWEGIAN FOREST CAT

BLACK TORTOISESHELL NORWEGIAN FOREST CAT

SILVER TABBY AND WHITE NORWEGIAN FOREST CAT

BLACK SMOKE AND WHITE NORWEGIAN FOREST CAT

chariot of the Norse goddess, Freya! In Norse fairy tales collected and written down in the 19th century, a 'fairy-cat' with a long, bushy tail often appears.

From a race of hardy outdoor cats used for hunting vermin on farms, a group of breeders began to develop the pedigree breed in the 1930s. At least one Norwegian

BROWN TABBY AND WHITE NORWEGIAN FOREST CAT

BLACK MACKEREL TABBY NORWEGIAN FOREST CAT

91

**BLACK-AND-WHITE
NORWEGIAN FOREST CAT**

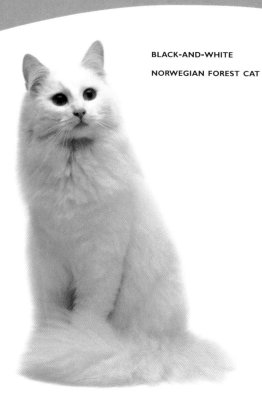

BLUE-EYED WHITE NORWEGIAN FOREST CAT

Forest Cat was shown in Oslo, Norway, before World War II, but planned breeding did not begin in earnest until the 1970s. The breed arrived in the US in 1979, and in Britain in the 1980s. There are now some 400 registered Forest Cats in Norway, and many more abroad, especially in neighbouring Sweden. While large and strong, Norwegian Forest Cats should never appear stocky and the face should be angular, giving a fine impression of alertness and intelligence, rather than of 'sweetness'! All colours are permitted – no points are allocated to coat colour in the scoring system at shows – more important is the quality of the coat. Tabbies and bicolours, however, predominate in the breed, reflecting the random bred cat population from which the Wegie is descended.

CREAM SMOKE WHITE NORWEGIAN FOREST CAT

Siberian Forest Cat

These cats are very similar in appearance to the Norwegian Forest Cat (see page 89) and, like them, have a wonderfully thick, dense and oily coat ideally suited for the extreme cold of a northern climate. It's likely that this breed has existed for thousands of years, independently of man. Russian cats were shown at early cat shows arranged by Harrison Weir – who, in fact, owned one himself – but the breed was largely forgotten during the 20th century when relationships between the Soviet Union and the rest of the world cooled. Recently, however, there has been an increasing interest in formalising the breed. Siberians were imported into the United States in 1990, thanks to the efforts of Elizabeth Terrell of the Starpoint Cattery – a name that can be found in the pedigrees of most of the top Siberians in America.

As interest in the Siberian grew, a greater variety of coat colours and patterns has been introduced, but some Russian clubs fear that cats exported for breeding in the West are not always the best. The face of the Siberian Forest Cat in Russia is different to that accepted in the West. In Russia a more 'wildcat' appearance is preferred, with a broad face and slightly tilted eyes giving it a more Asiatic cast. Outside

Date of origin: **1980s**
Place of origin: **Eastern Russia**
Ancestry: **household and farm cats**
Other names: **none**
Colours: **in Russia, the Siberian is allowed in only black- and red-based colours. Elsewhere a wider range of colours is recognised:**
　　Self (solid) colours and Tortie: black, red, blue, cream, tortoiseshell and blue tortie
　　Smoked, Shaded and Tipped colours: as for self and tortie
　　Tabbies, Silver Tabbies (Classic, Mackerel, Spotted): brown, red, blue, cream, tortie and blue tortie.
　　Bicolours: all allowed self, tortie and tabby colours with white
Coat length: **long**
Type of fur: **dense, waterproof undercoat, with long, coarse guard hairs to shed rain and snow**
Size: **4.5–9 kg (10–20 lb)**

Russia, the TICA standard for the Siberian head is less markedly wild – here the impression should be of 'roundness and circles' with a sweet expression and almost-round eyes. Furthermore, in its homeland, the Siberian is permitted in only black- and red-based colours to preserve its wild appearance. Consequently, the Siberian Forest Cat is developing two distinct looks internationally.

SILVER, TABBY AND WHITE SIBERIAN

The Siberian Forest Cat is a strong cat with a long, well-muscled and powerful body and sturdy legs, ending in large, round and fur-tufted paws. In both sexes, the hind legs are slightly longer than the forelegs when straight, and the body is carried with a slightly arched spine. Around the neck is a ruff, enhancing the short, sturdy proportions. The ears are medium in size, with rounded tips that are angled outwards, giving the cat an ever-alert appearance. Between the ears the head is broad and flat. The magnificent tail is thick, with a rounded tip while the hind quarters are shaggy. The topcoat is strong and slightly oily to shed rain and snow, while the dense woolly undercoat is thick enough to keep out the Arctic winds of Siberia. Every aspect of the Siberian Forest Cat demonstrates that it is designed to survive in the toughest conditions and climate on earth.

RED MACKEREL TABBY AND WHITE SIBERIAN

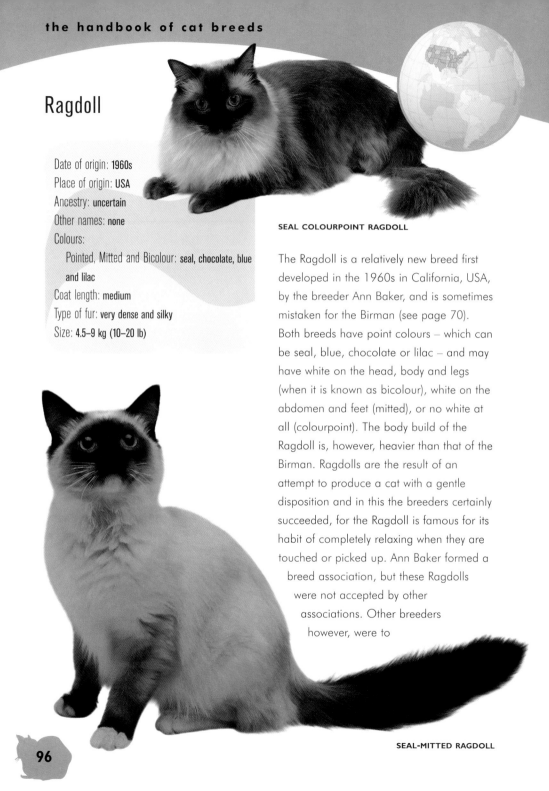

Ragdoll

Date of origin: 1960s
Place of origin: USA
Ancestry: uncertain
Other names: none
Colours:
    Pointed, Mitted and Bicolour: seal, chocolate, blue and lilac
Coat length: medium
Type of fur: very dense and silky
Size: 4.5–9 kg (10–20 lb)

SEAL COLOURPOINT RAGDOLL

The Ragdoll is a relatively new breed first developed in the 1960s in California, USA, by the breeder Ann Baker, and is sometimes mistaken for the Birman (see page 70). Both breeds have point colours – which can be seal, blue, chocolate or lilac – and may have white on the head, body and legs (when it is known as bicolour), white on the abdomen and feet (mitted), or no white at all (colourpoint). The body build of the Ragdoll is, however, heavier than that of the Birman. Ragdolls are the result of an attempt to produce a cat with a gentle disposition and in this the breeders certainly succeeded, for the Ragdoll is famous for its habit of completely relaxing when they are touched or picked up. Ann Baker formed a breed association, but these Ragdolls were not accepted by other associations. Other breeders however, were to

SEAL-MITTED RAGDOLL

BLUE-MITTED RAGDOLL

produce the breed of Ragdolls accepted today by the major registries. In addition, the Ragdoll was the first breed of cat in history to receive its own trademark!

The first Ragdolls were bred from a white, probably non-pedigree, long-haired queen called Josephine, and a Birman, or Birman-type tom called Daddy Warbucks. According to Ann Baker, Josephine had been severely injured – her pelvis was broken after she was hit by a car – and when she picked up the Ragdoll kittens they went limp in her hands. This led to the claim that Ragdolls were unable to feel pain or fear or to fight other animals, and that this trait was a direct result of Josephine's accident. That Ragdolls feel no pain is a myth – they have the same pain threshold as other cats – but they do indeed have a very docile nature, making them ideal and loving pets.
They are also an easy

breed to train because they respond extremely well to tasty treats as rewards! These characteristics are actually the result of genetic mutations in the selective breeding process among highly domesticated animals. Breeders also point out that all the varieties known as Ragdolls

CREAM-MITTED RAGDOLL (NEW COLOUR)

97

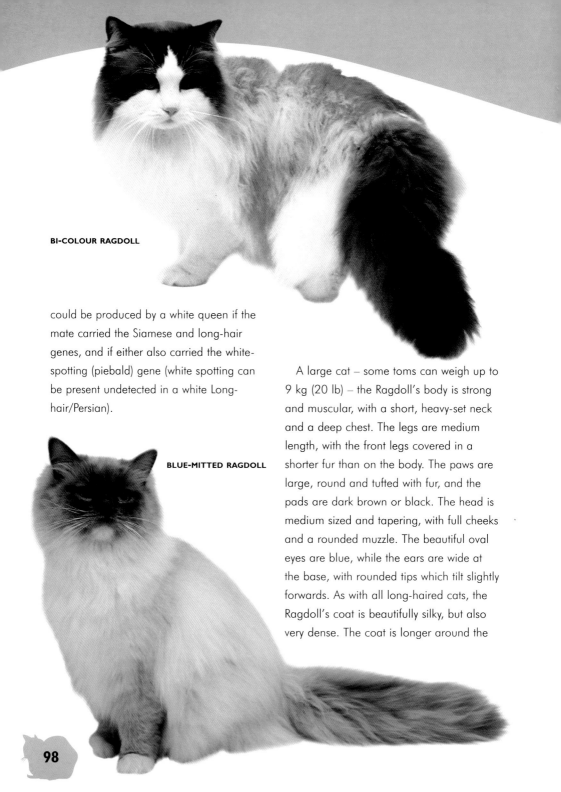

BI-COLOUR RAGDOLL

could be produced by a white queen if the mate carried the Siamese and long-hair genes, and if either also carried the white-spotting (piebald) gene (white spotting can be present undetected in a white Long-hair/Persian).

BLUE-MITTED RAGDOLL

A large cat – some toms can weigh up to 9 kg (20 lb) – the Ragdoll's body is strong and muscular, with a short, heavy-set neck and a deep chest. The legs are medium length, with the front legs covered in a shorter fur than on the body. The paws are large, round and tufted with fur, and the pads are dark brown or black. The head is medium sized and tapering, with full cheeks and a rounded muzzle. The beautiful oval eyes are blue, while the ears are wide at the base, with rounded tips which tilt slightly forwards. As with all long-haired cats, the Ragdoll's coat is beautifully silky, but also very dense. The coat is longer around the

SEAL TORTOISESHELL POINT RAGDOLL

neck, but short over the shoulders, and medium length on the sides, abdomen and hind legs.

Ragdolls are essentially pointed cats, born white and slowly developing their colours and patterns over the first two years. In the early years of the breed, the seal point and its dilute, blue, were the most common colours to be found in Ragdolls, but later breeders succeeded in producing chocolate and lilac colours. The breed standards recognise the usual markings for bicolours and colourpoints, but require good contrast, and the body colour on Ragdolls can be deeper than that accepted on other pointed breeds.

BLUE COLOURPOINT RAGDOLL

SEAL BI-COLOUR RAGDOLL

99

Somali

Date of origin: **1963**
Place of origin: **Canada and the USA**
Ancestry: **Abyssinian**
Other names: **Long-haired Abyssinian**
Colours:
   Tabbies (Ticked): **usual (called ruddy in the US), chocolate, sorrel (red), blue, lilac, fawn and cream**
   Torties: **usual tortie, chocolate, sorrel, blue, lilac and fawn tortie**
   Silver Tabbies (Ticked): **colours as for tabbies and torties, but must have white chests and underparts**
Coat length: **medium-long, with ruff and full breeches**
Type of fur: **Fine and silky, ticked (at least three and up to 12 bands of colour on each hair)**
Size: **3.5–5.5 kg (8–12 lb)**

USUAL SOMALI (CALLED RUDDY IN THE US)

With its beautiful shaggy coat, fluffy 'trousers' or breeches, exaggerated ear tufts and a fine, full tail like a fox's brush, the Somali is a wild-looking cat, vigorous and athletic. Yet, like their Abyssinian relations, Somalis are very gentle in nature, soft in voice and make for great companions.

This breed of cat was named after Somalia, a country next to Ethiopia (formerly known as Abyssinia), in order to emphasise the breed's similarity to the Abyssinian. In fact, the Somali is the long-haired variety of the short-haired Abyssinian.

At first, the Somali was not recognised by the registries because it was believed that some out-crossing of Abyssinians to long-haired breeds must have taken place. In fact, certain breeding lines of Abyssinians are now known to have carried the recessive (*l*) long hair gene (see pages 49–53) for many generations – long-haired kittens had appeared occasionally in Abyssinian litters in the UK and, in the 1940s, breeder Janet Robertson exported 'Abys' to North America and Australia, where descendants of these Abys also produced long-haired kittens. In the 1960s, Canadian breeder Ken McGill produced the first official Somali and, from his stock, the breed was fully developed in the US in the 1970s. The breed appeared in Europe in the 1980s and by 1991 had received worldwide recognition.

Like its Abyssinian forebears, the Somali has the same ticked coat, although it is silkier, softer and very much longer. Instead of two or three bands of ticking on each hair, the Somali can have up to 12 bands. The colouring, which may be 'usual' – called 'ruddy' in the US – or sorrel (red), is deeper and much richer. The usual or ruddy colour was one of the first to be

BLUE/SILVER SOMALI

accepted for showing. Here, the base coat is a red-brown shade of apricot while the ticking is black. On all Somalis, the ticking is much darker on the ground coat and, in autumn and winter when the Somali is in glorious full coat, they produce a beautiful, vibrant shimmer. The coat is full, but not woolly, and a full ruff around the neck is typical of the breed. It takes a long time for the coat and colouring to develop fully:

kittens are born very dark and only achieve a full ticked ruddy colouring at about 18 months.

Lithe and muscular in build, the Somali's legs are long, with oval–shaped, tufted paws. The head is a moderate wedge shape, and all Somalis have dark-rimmed eyes – as if they have been outlined in kohl or eyeliner – surrounded by 'spectacles' of lighter hair. On the cheeks and forehead

CHOCOLATE SOMALI

BLUE SOMALI

there are clear tabby markings — it is said the prophet Mohammed once embraced a tabby cat and, in so doing, left his initial 'M' on its forehead!

Since the long hair gene (*l*) is recessive, Somalis always breed true for long hair. Crossed with an Abyssinian, however, a Somali will have short-haired kittens carrying the gene for long hair. These offspring will have a much plusher coat than most 'normal' Abyssinians. Mated together, they will result in both long-haired and short-haired offspring. Notwithstanding, all 'short-haired Somalis' must be registered in North America as Somalis, even though they are genetically identical to many Abyssinians that may also be carrying the long-hair gene!

Tiffannie

Date of origin: 1980s

Place of origin: Britain

Ancestry: Burmese-Chinchilla crosses

Other names: none (not to be confused with the Tiffany, US appellation for the Chantilly)

Colours:

Self (solid) and sepia colours: black, chocolate, red, blue, lilac, cream, caramel and apricot

Torties: black, chocolate, blue, lilac and caramel torties

Shaded colours: as for self and sepia

Tabbies (solid, sepia, all patterns): brown, chocolate, red, blue, lilac, cream, caramel, apricot, Black tortie, chocolate, blue, lilac and caramel tortie

Coat length: long, with ruff at neck

Type of fur: very fine

Size: 3.5–6.5 kg (8–14 lb)

The attractive – and attractively named – Tiffannie are unusual for combining long, silky hair with the shaded tones of the colours of the Burmese (see page 170). Although it is sometimes confused with its US namesake – the Tiffany (elsewhere called Chantilly) – the Tiffannie has nothing to do with the breed. Instead, the Tiffannie is essentially a long-haired Burmese and is the only Asian long-haired cat. Born a pale café au lait colour, the subtle sable colouring and long coat develop only gradually and the colour generally remains lighter than in a Burmese cat of the same age. Like all kittens, the Tiffannie is born with blue eyes, but these change to grey then to the adult golden colour.

The Tiffannie's origins can be traced back to an accidental mating in London, England, in 1981, between a Chinchilla Long-hair/Persian and a lilac Burmese which belonged to Baroness Miranda von Kirchberg. The first generation were short-haired, shaded Burmillas (see page 179) but subsequent generations ultimately revealed the recessive long-hair and sepia-pointing genes. Although the breed was developed with the assistance of Burmese breeders, the two breeds remain distinct.

While their coat is semi-long, very fine and silky, as one would expect in the offspring of a Persian/Long-hair, the body

BLUE SHADED SILVER TIFFANIE

retains the Burmese conformation: a medium-sized, muscular body with a round chest and straight back. The head is a short wedge, with a distinct nose break in profile, while the medium-sized ears continue the lines of the face. Eyes are neither almond-shaped, nor round and are set slightly obliquely. The legs are medium long and the paws rounded, while the tail is long and elegantly plumed. In temperament, the Tiffannie has combined the characteristics of its parent breeds once again to great effect – they are more lively than the average Long-hair/Persian, yet less boisterous than the average Burmese! The breed standard for the Tiffannie does, in fact, place emphasis on good temperament. This, combined with low maintenance in a long-haired cat, will undoubtedly ensure that the delightful and beguiling Tiffannie will become an even more popular breed worldwide.

CHOCOLATE/SMOKE TIFFANIE

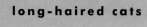

Long-hair/Persian

Longhairs/Persians are both an important part of the pedigree cat world – having appeared regularly in shows for well over one hundred years – and greatly prized as pets by owners worldwide. The long coat is the result of the recessive gene (*l*) (see pages 49–53) and the most likely place of origin was Asia Minor, where, according to legend, the Persian cat was created by a magician from a little flicker of fire, the spark of two distant stars and a swirl of grey smoke.

Date of origin: **1800s**
Place of origin: **Britain**
Ancestry: **Middle-eastern longhairs**
Other names: **called Persian in the USA**
Colours: **see main text**
Coat length: **up to 10 cm (4 in) long**
Type of fur: **soft and thick but not woolly**
Size: **3.5–7 kg (8–15 lb)**

RED PERSIAN

BLUE CREAM PERSIAN

107

CREAM PERSIAN

In 1876, long-haired cats were referred to as 'Asiatic cats', but they had been seen in Europe some 300 years before this.

BLACK PERSIAN

CREAM POINT PERSIAN

BROWN PATCHED TABBY PERSIAN

Today, most cats of the long-hair type are known as Long-haired in Britain, where only selfs are called Longhairs (each colour is classified as a separate breed, of which there are nearly 50!) In the USA, these cats are known as Persians and the colours are listed as varieties which, for show purposes, are divided into five divisions: solid (self), shaded, smoke/tabby, part-coloured and point-restricted colours. Nevertheless, the ideal body type is pretty much the same — a big, cobby body, low on the legs, with a round, broad head, full cheeks, large,

BLACK SMOKE PERSIAN

109

WHITE PERSIAN

round eyes and small, rounded ears and, of course, the beautiful, long, silky and full coat. While the early Persians/Longhairs had short, compact faces, they were not the flat faces seen today. European breeders still prefer what they term a 'moderate' nose, while American breeders and many show judges look for the flatter, or 'ultra-type' face. This trend reached its most extreme in the 'Peke-faced' Persian/Long-hair where the narrow nostrils and restricted tear ducts caused by this face shape meant that these cats often suffered for their appearance. This look is no longer desired by many breeders today.

When Harrison Weir set out standards for

TORTOISESHELL PERSIAN

CHINCHILLA PERSIAN

cat varieties in the late 19th century, the colours he described in Persians/Longhairs were white, black, blue, grey, red and any other self colour, with brown, blue, silver, light grey and white for tabbies. By 1901, the recognised colours in Britain were black, white, blue, orange, cream, sable, smoke, tabby, spotted, chinchilla, tortoiseshell, bicolour and tricolour. The orange Persians/Longhairs were the ancestors of the red self colours and red tabbies, and the tricolours were most likely tortie-and-white.

The self colour group of Persians/Longhairs today includes whites, blacks, blues, chocolates, lilacs, reds and creams. While black – listed as Breed Number 1 in the UK – is the oldest variety of all, in 1910 there were in fact only 10 registered individuals. It was not until the end of World War II, when American breeders 'rescued' the breed, that black Persians/Longhairs became significant in numbers. The white selfs were among the very first long-haired cats in Europe, renowned then as now, for their blue eyes, but also for their deafness, which is associated with the dominant white gene W (see pages 49–53). Due to the way this gene acts, some white Persian/ Long-haired kittens show small clusters of coloured hairs on their heads,

BROWN TABBY PERSIAN

SEAL TORTOISESHELL COLOURPOINT PERSIAN

be free from tabby markings – and the long coat does help obscure some of the 'tabbiness'. A truly unmarked red Persian/Long-hair is probably an impossibility, due to the way the orange gene (O) works.

Tabbies have always been bred by cat lovers and, in 1871, they were included in the classification for the first famous cat show held by Weir in London. Today, both the mackerel (lined) and classic (blotched) tabby patterns are recognised in North America, while in the UK, only the classic type – termed

revealing the underlying colour genotype and giving an idea of what the kitten would have looked like without the action of the recessive white gene. Today, deafness is selectively bred against by careful cross-breeding using coloured Persians and by neutering deaf kittens.

Blue has always been one of the most popular varieties – a trend said to have been set by Queen Victoria, who was inseparable from her two Blues – and Blues now even have shows dedicated solely to them!

The rarest of all the self Persian/Longhairs is the red self, which was originally called orange. Such cats are difficult to breed to perfection – although show standards require red selfs to

TABBY COLOURPOINT PERSIAN

BLUE TABBY PERSIAN

simply 'tabby' – competes. These tabbies continue to be bred in the basic colours, such as brown (i.e. genetically black), which is both the original colour and essentially the natural tabby, along with silvers and reds while, more recently, newer colours and patterns have been introduced, such as 'shaded cameos' in red, cream, cream-shell (essentially a cream chinchilla) blue-cream and tortie.

The fall of the breed's long coat makes a great display for tortoiseshell colouring. The first torties classified were standard black and reds, but soon red Persians/Longhairs were mated with blues and the blue-creams, or blue torties appeared. Tortie-and-whites were once called 'chintz cats' – and are still known today as 'Calicoes' in the US because of their resemblance to the bright patterns on printed calico cotton – while the original bicoloured cats (black,

blue, red and cream) were known as 'magpie cats'. The ideal pattern for the bicolour Persian/Long-hair, which is well known in fancy-bred mice and rabbits, is called the 'Dutch coat' pattern, where the white areas are confined to the underparts. In bicolour Persians/Longhairs, this perfect marking is very difficult to achieve and, consequently, some flexibility is allowed. A distinct variant in patterns – though genetically the same as the bicolour – is the Van Pattern: a white body and legs, with a coloured tail and face markings not extending below the level of the eyes or beyond the base of the ears.

Shaded and Tipped Persian/Long-hair varieties developed out of the early silver tabbies and the best-known member of this group is undoubtedly the Silver Chinchilla – most often called simply, Chinchilla. One of the earliest and most famous chinchillas was called Silver Lambkin and it seems that he gave rise to both silver and golden kittens. The silver variety was what breeders were aiming for, and the golden was ignored for some time because some breeders maintained they were the result of 'illegal' or accidental matings between self-coloured Persians/Longhairs and Chinchillas. Shaded Silvers (called 'pewter' in the UK) and shaded goldens are similar to the Chinchillas, except that the degree of tipping is greater, so the colours appear much darker. The Shaded Silver is recognised in the US as a black-tipped cat with green or blue-green eyes, and in red and tortoiseshell versions

RED COLOURPOINT PERSIAN

DILUTE CALICO, BLUE TORTOISESHELL AND WHITE TABBY PERSIAN

(called shaded cameo and shaded tortoiseshell) while in Britain, only the black versions are recognised (as pewters) with orange or copper eyes. The Golden Persian, which has deep tipping on an apricot base, looks like a golden version of the Shaded Silver (Pewter) and is one of the most recent, and most attractive, varieties of the Persian/Long-hair breeds, even though the genetics of this colour are still disputed.

RED TABBY PERSIAN

BLUE CREAM PERSIAN

115

BLUE COLOURPOINT PERSIAN

Whatever colour or pattern, the Persian/Long-hair are famous for their long, silky coats, which require daily grooming to keep them looking like a supreme champion which, to their owners, each cat is. The daily grooming routine is not only enjoyed by the cat, but helps to cement the very special bond between the cat and its owner – a very strong relationship for which this breed and its owners are well known! Furthermore, if the owner takes a little time to groom, the Persian/Long-hair will not swallow so much of its own hair, thus avoiding fur balls, which can block the intestines. One of the quietest and least active of the breeds of cat, they are generally regarded as indoor cats. But this does not mean that Persians/Longhairs don't enjoy outdoor activity – they display the same feline characteristics when guarding their territory or hunting as any other breeds.

TORTOISESHELL AND WHITE PERSIAN

Scottish Fold

Date of origin: **1961**

Place of origin: **Scotland**

Ancestry: **farm cats, British and American Shorthairs**

Other names: **Highland Fold**

Colours: **all colours and patterns including pointed, sepia and mink**

Coat length: **can be long-or short-coated**

Type of fur: **soft and dense, standing away from the body in the long-hair**

Size: **2.5–6 kg (6–13 lb)**

SHADED SILVER SCOTTISH FOLD

While folded ears are common among dog breeds, in cats they are rare. All Scottish Folds can be traced back to Susie, a white farm cat born in Tayside, Scotland. Two years later, Susie bore two more folded-ear kittens, one of which, a white female, was given to a local shepherd, William Ross, and his wife Mary and named Snooks. The uniqueness of the 'abnormality' was noticed and soon a breeding programme was established with the help of two geneticists, Pat Turner and Pete Dyte. It was discovered that Susie carried the dominant long-hair gene (*l*) (see pages 49–53), which could also be carried in any short-haired offspring, only appearing in later generations. Long-haired Scottish Folds, however, are still rare.

CALICO SCOTTISH FOLD

The short-hair variety can trace its ancestry back to Snooks, who was mated with a British Shorthair (see page 130) and produced Snowball, a white male. In 1971, Mary Ross sent some of her Folds to geneticist Neil Todd in Newtonville, Massachusetts, where further breeding developments using British and American Shorthairs (see page 138) continued. The main centre for breeding is still in the US.

Scottish Folds must be mated to cats with normal ears otherwise any homozygous (Fold-to-Fold mated) offspring may suffer from deformities of the joints and cartilage that start to become evident when the kitten reaches four to six months old. The cause of these deformities is something of a mystery since they affect only a proportion of cats, including those Folds that are heterozygous (Fold-to-Other-Breed mated). In long-haired Folds especially, the deformities may go unnoticed under their beautiful coats, so checking long-haired kittens' tails for thickening joints is vital.

The folded ears are the result of a dominant gene that is responsible for varying degrees of fold. They are present from birth, but the extent of folding may not become fully apparent until the kitten matures. The original Scottish Fold, Susie, had what is now called a 'single fold', where the ears bend forwards. Today's show cats have 'triple folds' where the ears are folded tightly and flat against the head, set according to the breed standards 'in a cap-like fashion' to expose a rounded cranium'. The head is indeed well–rounded, and the shape is further enhanced by the prominent cheeks, whisker pads and large, rounded eyes.

Like the Scots themselves, Scottish Folds are robust, strong and seemingly impervious to the cold! They are also highly resistant to many common feline diseases. Though placid cats, and perhaps a little 'reserved' or undemonstrative, they are good natured. Their 'sad' look is too often misinterpreted as an indicator of their inner feelings!

Coupari

Date of origin: 1960s

Place of origin: Scotland

Ancestry: Scottish Fold (short haired variety), domestic and farm cats

Other names: Scottish Fold Long-hair (American CFA), Highland Fold (American ACFA)

Colours: all colours and patterns including pointed, sepia and mink

Coat length: medium-long

Type of fur: Soft and dense, standing away from the body

Size: 2.4–6 kg (6–13 lb)

The Coupari is one of the names given to the long-haired variety of the Scottish Fold (see page 117). The name is derived from the home of the founding cat in Coupar Angus in Scotland. In the American CFA, the Coupari is called the Scottish Fold Long-hair; while in the American ACFA, it is known as the Highland Fold – despite the fact that Coupar Angus is not in the Scottish Highlands, which causes some mirth among Scottish breeders in particular!

SEAL TABBY POINT COUPARI

Both long- and short-haired varieties are distinguished by the folded ears – but these do not appear until kittens are about three weeks old – but straight (normal) eared kittens are also produced because the folded ear is the product of an incomplete gene and is the result of spontaneous mutation. Consequently both Scottish folds – the short-haired variety – and Couparis – the long haired variety – are still very rare. Cats with 'folded' ears have been known for centuries, but all Couparis and Scottish Folds can trace their ancestry back to Susie, a white farm cat born in 1961 on a farm in Coupar Angus, in the Tayside region of Scotland, northwest of Dundee. Susie was 'discovered' by William and Mollie Ross, who asked the original owners if they could have one of the kittens and proceeded to develop the breed.

Genetic studies by Pat Turner and Peter Dyte in the 1960s discovered that Susie also carried the gene for long hair: this could be carried in short-haired offspring and could appear in later generations. While the short-haired Scottish Fold was to find successful out crosses in British and American Shorthairs (see pages 130–42), long-haired out crosses were absent, until it was discovered that the prick-eared Scottish

Vannant had all the same genes for the breed type – except for the folded ears. The Scottish Vannant can thus be successfully mated to both a Scottish Fold and a Coupari, to produce both short- and long-haired cats with folded ears. This avoids the dangers of breeding 'fold-to-fold' which may produce litters with inherited osteodystrophy. Nevertheless, the Coupari and its short-haired cousin still remain quite rare.

In 1983, when the Cat Association of Britain was formed, one of the first new breeds to gain Championship status was the Scottish Fold, and the following year the Coupari was also accepted for competition. Breeders in the UK today are united in the Scottish Breeds Association. In the USA the Coupari is a Championship breed, while in the UK it has medalist titles. Although it is not (as yet) eligible itself for titles, the Scottish Vannant can be shown in the class for new breeds.

American Curl

Date of origin: 1981
Place of origin: USA
Ancestry: American household cats
Other names: none
Colours: all self and tortie colours, all patterns of smoke, shaded and tipped, tabbies and Silver tabbies
Bicolours: classic and Van
Self, Tabby (lynx) and Tortie point
Coat length: medium to long (long-haired variety)
Type of fur: silky with minimal undercoat, so lying close to body in both long- and short-haired varieties
Size: 3–5 kg (7–11 lb)

The American Curl breed includes both long- and short-coat types. The short-haired American Curl has taken slightly longer to develop because the original Curls were all long-haired and many short-haired Curls carry the hidden long-hair gene and produce long-haired kittens. The American Curl is best known not for its coat, but for the mutation which causes the ears of these cats to curl backwards, creating its highly distinctive appearance.

BROWN TABBY AND WHITE AMERICAN CURL

The Curl has three grades: cats with their ears just turned back (first degree) are called American Curl Straight Ears and become household pets, those with a 50% curl (second degree) are used for breeding and those with full crescents (third degree) are shown competitively. The kittens are born with normal-looking ears and typically half the litter will develop the curl at about a week old, continuing to develop over several months. In spite of their appearance, even third-degree-curled ears can be swivelled around by the cat like any other normal-eared cat!

The ancestry of the breed is unknown, although in 1981 a stray, black, long-haired kitten, with unusual, curled ears found herself a new home with Grace and Joe Ruga in Lakeland, California. The Rugas named the kitten Shulamith, which means 'peaceful one', after the shepherdess in the *Song of Songs*, and all Curls – whether long- or short-haired – today trace their origin back to her.

In December 1981, Shulamith had a litter of four kittens, two of which had the same curly ears. The Rugas realised that a new breed could be established because the trait was dominant. The cats were first shown in 1983 in California, and they were soon formally recognised in the US with the first American Curls reaching the UK in 1995.

AMERICAN CURL, BROWN CLASSIC

Nevertheless, the American Curl has established itself as a popular cat, not only for its dramatic face – often described as 'pixie–like', enhanced by walnut-shaped and slightly tilted eyes – but for its lively, friendly and independent spirit. Semi-foreign in build, with moderate muscles, the Curl has sturdy legs, a little bowed at the front, with the hind legs slightly longer in length. This is set off in the long-haired Curl by a magnificently plumed tail, and in the shorthair by a tail that equals the length of the body, wide at the base and tapering to the tip. The show standards for short-haired American Curls differ from their long-haired cousins only in coat length.

BROWN CLASSIC AMERICAN CURL

124

Short-haired Breeds

THE BURMESE IS A CLASSIC SHORT—HAIRED BREED

When, thousands of years ago, domestic cats spread from Egypt across the world, new varieties evolved to suit the local climate and terrain. In northern climates, cats developed stocky, cobby bodies and thicker coats, while those cats which spread eastwards across Asia, developed thinner coats and smaller bodies to help them lose excess heat in warmer climates. In the wild, short hair is normal in cats. It is only in the extreme cold of regions such as Siberia, the home of the Siberian Tiger, that longer hair is found on wild cats. Short fur is much easier to keep clean and pest- and tangle-free and is also genetically dominant. There are many types of short-hair coats in cats, ranging from the silky-soft, fine fur of the Rex to the dense coat of the Manx.

There are three main categories of short-haired cats: British (and European), American, and Foreign (or Oriental). The British Shorthair is a cobby with strong, short legs, a short, dense coat, a broad, round head, round eyes and superb

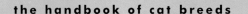

THE SLEEK LINES OF THE ORIENTAL SHORT—HAIR
MAKE THIS A VERY POPULAR BREED.

colouring. There are only slight differences
between the British and European
Shorthairs, but since 1982 they have been
recognised as separate breeds. Over the
years since it was established as a breed,
the European Shorthair has become less
cobby than the British type, with a slightly
longer body. Both do, however, display the
same basic traits of being a strong, hardy
cat with a beautiful coat and a calm,
affectionate personality.

THE AMERICAN SHORT—HAIR
IS A VERY POPULAR BREED

THE AMERICAN SHORT—HAIR IS GENERALLY
LARGER THAN ITS BRITISH/EUROPEAN AND
ORIENTAL COUNTERPARTS.

The Romans were said to have introduced domestic cats to northern Europe some 2,000 years ago, so it is not surprising that when breeding and exhibiting cats at shows became popular in the 19th century, British and European breeders concentrated their attentions on their native cats.

THE ORIENTAL SHORT—HAIR HAS VERY DISTINCTIVE SHAPED HEAD AND EYES.

AN ATHLETIC BREED, AMERICAN SHORT—HAIRS HAVE LONGER LEGS THAN OTHER BREEDS.

127

**THE SIAMESE IS ONE OF THE MOST WIDELY
RECOGNISED AND BEST—LOVED OF ALL BREEDS.**

The pure-bred American Shorthair is a larger and more athletic cat with longer legs and a more oblong-shaped head. Some consider the pure-bred American Shorthair to be closer in body type to its non-pedigree counterpart, but a pure-bred anima – the result of generations of selective breeding – will have a body, coat and colouring that represent the very highest standards of quality.

The Foreign, or Oriental, Shorthair, looks completely different to its occidental cousins. These are slender-bodied cats with long, slim legs, the characteristic wedge-shaped head and long, pointed ears, and the very distinctive, slanting eyes.

At the first cat shows held in the 19th century, short-haired breeds had pride of place as few Siamese cats had been imported. By the end of the century, however, the situation had changed markedly as Long-haired, or Persian, cats had become immensely popular and begun to outnumber the shorthairs at shows by 4 to 1. These long-haired cats with the luxurious, slinky coats and the appeal of originating in faraway parts of the world meant that a short-haired kitten has never since fetched the price commanded by a Persian one.

Nevertheless, the native short-haired breeds of Britain, Europe and North America, have many advantages as domestic companions. They have a hardiness and stamina born of countless generations of life in all climates, and temperamentally, they are ideally suited to family life – being less excitable and easy to groom.

BRITISH (SHOWN HERE) AND EUROPEAN SHORT–HAIRS ARE HARDY BREEDS.

THE EXOTIC SHORT–HAIR IS A RELATIVELY NEW BREED, AND SHARES CHARACTERISTICS OF BOTH LONG AND SHORT–HAIRED BREEDS.

British Shorthair

Date of origin: 1880s

Place of origin: Britain

Ancestry: household, farm and street cats

Other names: tipped colours were once known as Chinchilla Shorthairs

Colours:

Self (solid) colours: white, cream, blue, blue-cream, black, chocolate, lilac and red

Tabby (Classic, Mackerel, and Spotted – or blotched – markings): silver, brown, red, cream and blue

Spotted: red, brown, silver or any other tabby colour

Tortoiseshell: tortoiseshell, blue-cream tortie, chocolate tortie and lilac tortie.

Bicolour: all self and tortie colours with white

Smoke and Tipped: colours as for self and tortie

Colourpoint: all self, tortie and tabby colours

Coat length: short

Type of fur: dense and springy, 'breaks' over joints

Size: 4–8 kg (9–18 lb)

LILAC TORTIE BRITISH SHORTHAIR

All the European cat breeds suffered during World War II, but some say that the British Shorthair suffered the most. In the immediate post-war years there were very few pedigree stud males left and, as a result, some breeders mated their cats to shorthairs of foreign body type, which nearly led to the cobby build being lost. In the 1950s, breeders reversed the trend by mating to large-built, blue Persians. While this did restore the breed's qualities, it also meant that some kittens had longer, softer coats, and a more Persian head shape. The show standards set for British and European Shorthairs specifies a straight nose – a difficult feat to achieve using Persian ancestry, even when the Persians bred in

Europe are not as snub- or 'peke-nosed' as those in America. One rare trait separates the British Shorthair breed from most short-haired cats: about half of all British Shorthairs have Type B blood.

In the early days of the breed, the self colours of the British Shorthair were the most popular, probably because solid-coloured cats, with no markings, were less common in non-pedigree pets. Of the various self colours, the most highly prized was the blue – which is, in fact, a beautiful bluish-grey – and this has remained popular ever since. As a result the Blue British Shorthair is sometimes accorded solitary breed status as the 'British Blue' and is regarded as the epitome of the breed. As with all British Shorthairs, the ideal is a lovely, rounded face with full

BLACK SMOKE TORTIE BRITISH SHORTHAIR

cheeks, a cobby body with strong, broad shoulders, a deep chest and strong, short legs. The ears are small with rounded tips and set well apart. The nose is short and straight, with the nose pad corresponding to the coat colour. In self-coloured British Shorthairs, the well-rounded eyes are copper, deep orange or deep gold, except in the Blue- and Odd-eyed White. The Orange-Eyed White – which rarely suffers from the congenital deafness suffered by Blue- and Odd-Eyed Whites – was developed from the Blue-Eyed White, which appeared at the end of the 19th century, but a perfect white coat, with no yellow tinge is very rare.

BLUE SPOTTED BRITISH SHORTHAIR

CINNAMON SELF BRITISH SHORTHAIR

LILAC TORTIE BRITISH SHORTHAIR

LILAC TORTIE BRITISH SHORTHAIR

The cream British Shorthair, recognised since the 1920s, is one of the most difficult to breed in the ideal coat colour: a pale cream shade completely free of any tabby markings. Often the colour is too 'hot' (too red) and there are residual tabby-type bars on the tail and markings on the face.

Tortoiseshell cats are not rare, but they are also very difficult to breed to the breed standard, which calls for a mingling of colours without obvious patches, brindling or tabby markings. Both the nose leather and paw pads in torties must correspond with the coat colours. Even under the most 'favourable' circumstances a litter may contain only one tortie and, because the colour and sex of cats is genetically linked, torties are nearly always female — the rare, male tortie will be infertile. Tortie-and-Whites, known as Calicoes in the US, have distinct patches of red and black because, for some as-yet-unknown reason, the bicolour gene affects the red sex-linked gene making the mingled colours of the

BLUE/SILVER BRITISH SHORTHAIR

'pure' tortie unachievable in tortie-and-whites. The breed standard requires Tortie-and-Whites to have a colour balance in their coats of one-third to one-half white, as in other bicoloured cats.

The British Tabby Shorthair, whether classic, mackerel or spotted (botched) has complete rings on the tail and even bars on the legs. The original tabby was the Brown and is less commonly seen today. Soon after, the Reds made their appearance on the scene. Ginger-reds are common in non-pedigree cats in Britain, but a century of selective breeding means that a pedigree red tabby is a truly magnificent animal, far removed in richness of colour from the common 'ginger toms'. The word 'tabby' is said to be derived from the town of Attabiya, near Baghdad, in Iraq, which was famous for producing a watered silk cloth

BI-COLOURED BRITISH SHORTHAIR

WHITE BRITISH SHORTHAIR

133

BLACK BRITISH SHORTHAIR

known as 'tabbi silk', the pattern of which
was shared by local cats. On the tabby's
forehead is the 'M' mark – said to have
been left by the prophet Mohammed when
he embraced a cat! Like the self-coloured
British Shorthairs, tabbies have the same
copper-coloured eyes, except in the Silver
Tabby, which has green or hazel eyes.

TORTIE BRITISH SHORTHAIR

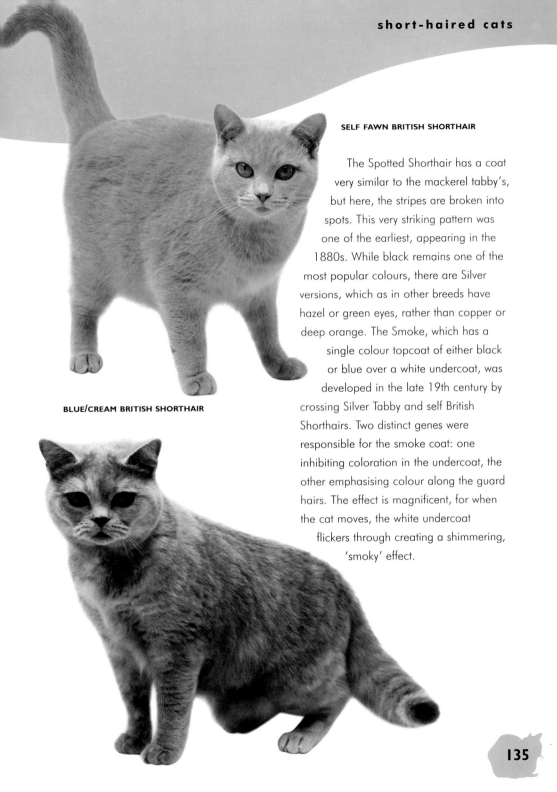

SELF FAWN BRITISH SHORTHAIR

The Spotted Shorthair has a coat very similar to the mackerel tabby's, but here, the stripes are broken into spots. This very striking pattern was one of the earliest, appearing in the 1880s. While black remains one of the most popular colours, there are Silver versions, which as in other breeds have hazel or green eyes, rather than copper or deep orange. The Smoke, which has a single colour topcoat of either black or blue over a white undercoat, was developed in the late 19th century by crossing Silver Tabby and self British Shorthairs. Two distinct genes were responsible for the smoke coat: one inhibiting coloration in the undercoat, the other emphasising colour along the guard hairs. The effect is magnificent, for when the cat moves, the white undercoat flickers through creating a shimmering, 'smoky' effect.

BLUE/CREAM BRITISH SHORTHAIR

135

**CREAM COLOURPOINT
BRITISH SHORTHAIR**

**BLACK/CHOCOLATE/LILAC
TORTIE BRITISH SHORTHAIR**

The British Colourpoint, as well as some other self colours, in British Shorthairs, are the result of out crossings to Foreign, or, Oriental, breeds. British Seal Colourpoint Shorthairs, while having the physical characteristics of other British Shorthairs, share their exotic coat pattern with Siamese, while the gene for the rich brown colour of the Chocolate self originally came from Oriental breeds, first introduced into the Longhair/Persian breed and then into the British Shorthair. The British Tipped Shorthair, which was known as the Chinchilla Shorthair until 1978, was developed through matings with Chinchilla Longhairs. In kittens, it is possible to see this long-hair ancestry because it is some months before they develop their adult coats. In some instances, these new coat colours are not accepted outside the UK.

RED SILVER SPOTTED BRITISH SHORTHAIR

BROWN SPOTTED BRITISH SHORTHAIR

As a breed, all British Shorthairs, whatever their colour or markings, are delightful cats that are intelligent, affectionate and, for want of another expression, 'cuddly' – their plump, round cheeks make tickling them very difficult to resist!

SILVER TABBY BRITISH SHORTHAIR

BLACK TIPPED BRITISH SHORTHAIR

137

American Shorthair

Date of origin: 1900s

Place of origin: USA

Ancestry: domestic cats

Other names: once known as Domestic Shorthair

Colours:

Self and Tortie: black, red, blue, cream, white, tortoiseshell and blue-cream

Smoke: black, cameo, blue, tortoiseshell and blue-cream

Shaded and Tipped: colours as for self and tortie, except white

Tabbies (Classic and mackerel): brown, red, blue, cream, brown patched, blue patched

Tabby Bicolour: all tabby colours with white

Shaded Tabbies: colours and patterns as for standard tabbies

Bicolour (Standards and Vans): as for self and tortie except white

Smoke, Shaded & Tipped Bicolour: black smoke, cameo smoke, blue smoke, tortoiseshell smoke, shaded cameo, shell cameo with white

Silver Tabby Bicolour: silver tabby, cameo tabby, silver patched tabby with white

Coat length: short

Type of fur: thick, quite hard

Size: 3.5-kg (8–15 lb)

**BROWN CLASSIC TABBY
AMERICAN SHORTHAIR**

It may be that the first domestic cats reached North America with the Pilgrim Fathers aboard the *Mayflower*. The non-pedigree cats of America, like their European cousins, certainly earned their keep as efficient pest controllers for over two centuries before a systematic, selective breeding and show programme was developed.

At the earliest cat shows, held in the north-eastern states in the 19th century, the gentle giants of the cat world, the long-haired Maine Coon dominated. However, the tough conditions and working environments of many of the American short-haired cats meant that these were – like the very people themselves – tough, resilient and resourceful. While in the early days of the breed, the lines were strengthened by matings with pedigree British Shorthairs, today the American Shorthair is a very distinctive breed of strong and hardy cats. With more natural predators around in the United States than in Europe, the American Shorthairs evolved into bigger cats than their continental cousins.

The history of the American Shorthair is said to date from around 1900 when a pedigree red tabby male – with the particularly feminine name of 'Belle' – was sent from England to America and was the first short-haired cat to be registered as a pedigree animal by the CFA. So the first American Shorthair was actually a British Shorthair émigré! Others soon followed Belle across the Atlantic to a new world, including a male Silver Tabby delightfully named 'Pretty Correct'. But American breeders were also starting to register their own cats. The first home-grown American Shorthair to be registered was 'Buster Brown', a male Black Smoke, said to have been born on 15 January, 1904.

At first, the breed was called simply the 'Shorthair', but soon it became known as the Domestic Shorthair – a name it is sometimes still called today, although officially it is called the American Shorthair – and bred in a huge range of magnificent colours and markings. Although no longer permitted, for a time any non-pedigree cat that met the standard could be registered, widening the gene pool of the breed. In 1971, one such cat was even declared American Shorthair of the year by the CFA. The CFA breed standard describes the American Shorthair as having 'no part of its anatomy so exaggerated as to foster weakness... The general effect is of the trained athlete'.

The body is solid, powerful and muscular, and less square in shape than the British Shorthair. The legs are of medium length (a little longer than the British), capable of high leaps and heavily muscled to cope with any terrain. The head is large, but slightly longer than it is wide, with full cheeks and large, rounded eyes that are very slightly tilted. The tail is medium length and thick at the base, and the coat is short and thick, with quite a hard texture to it – at shows, in fact, judges penalise exhibits for having soft, fluffy coats!

The best known American Shorthairs are undoubtedly the Silver Tabbies with their dense black markings on a silver background. In 1965, a Silver Tabby won the United States Cat of the Year award, and prompted the breed name to be changed from 'Domestic Shorthair' to the appropriately proud 'American Shorthair'.

While the CFA accepts only blotched and striped tabby patterns – markings that were prevalent among the breed's emigrant ancestors – the TICA accepts spotted and ticked patterns as well.

SILVER TABBY AMERICAN SHORTHAIR

Apart from their famous hardiness, American Shorthairs are noted for their easy-going temperament, their hunting abilities and their intelligence. Easy to rear and feed, they also make ideal house pets.

**CLASSIC SILVER TABBY
AMERICAN SHORTHAIR**

Exotic Shorthair

This exotic-looking breed is a 'short-haired long-hair' or, the short-haired version of the Long-hair/Persian (see page 107)! They have the compact body conformation of the Longhairs, along with its flattened, 'teddy-bear' face, but a rather original, dense, double coat that is not quite long and not quite short, but still needs twice-weekly combing to keep it in tiptop condition! The beautiful Exotic Shorthair is both a recently developed breed and one that is still quite rare, in part because many litters contain long-haired kittens.

For some years, breeders in North America out crossed American Shorthairs to Long-hair/Persians. In mid 1967, it was decided that a new breed name should be created for cats of mixed Long-hair/Persian

Date of origin: **1960s**
Place of origin: **USA**
Ancestry: **Long-hair and American Shorthair**
Other names: **none**
Colours: **all colours and patterns including sepia, pointed and mink**
Coat length: **medium – slightly longer than other shorthairs**
Type of fur: **a double coat that is soft and plush, and dense enough to stand slightly away from the body**
Size: **3–6.5 kg (7–14 lb)**

SILVER TIPPED EXOTIC SHORTHAIR

SELF BLACK EXOTIC SHORTHAIR

and American Shorthair ancestry to leave the American Shorthair breed free of cats with mixed ancestry. Consequently, the parents of an Exotic Shorthair must either be one Long-hair/Persian and one American Shorthair, two Exotic Shorthairs, or one Long-hair/Persian and one Exotic Shorthair. Whatever the original blend, the result is a cat that is round in shape from its ears to its toes, and perfect for cuddling! It's not the soft coat that makes the roundness though – underneath it are strong muscles

CREAM MACKEREL TABBY AND WHITE EXOTIC SHORTHAIR

that give the breed its curves!

Often described as 'chunky', the Exotic Shorthair has a medium to large, cobby body standing on short but firm legs. The head is large and round with full cheeks and a nose that is shorter than that of a British or American Shorthair. Because it has inherited some of the Long-hair/Persian 'flawed' characteristics, such as the overflowing tear ducts, constricted nostrils and dental problems, the British breed standard – in an effort to breed for health rather than appearance – calls for the nose leather of the Exotic Shorthair to be below the edge of the eye.

CREAM EXOTIC SHORTHAIR

Nevertheless, like many hybrids, the Exotic Shorthair is very hardy and combines the best of the parental breed-temperaments, making for an affectionate and relaxed cat.

An even coat is a show standard essential – judges find fault with the merest suggestion of feathery hair on the ears or tail along with any tufting on the toes. Exotic tabbies may be classic, mackerel or spotted – unlike Longhairs/Persians, which are only recognised in the classic pattern. The facial markings of all three patterns are the same with only the body marking varying. While the pointed pattern is a separate group in Longhairs/Persians, in the Exotic it is included in the colours. All points should be evenly matched, with the mask extending over the entire face. In the tortie Exotics, the standard calls for the colours to be balanced and softly intermingled, and for all four feet and the tail to contain both colours. Because tortie patterning is inherently difficult to predict and to breed, some distinct patches of colour are allowed, as are blazes of colour on the face.

BLACK SMOKE EXOTIC SHORTHAIR

145

Chartreux

Date of origin: **pre-18th century**
Place of origin: **France**
Ancestry: **household cats**
Other names: **none**
Colours: **blue self only**
Coat length: **short**
Type of fur: **dense and glossy**
Size: **3–7.5 kg (7–17 lb)**

It is possibly that the Chartreux's ancestors came from Syria and were taken by ship to France in the Middle Ages. References to the breed date back as far as 1558. They were said to have been bred by the Carthusian monks at the monastery of La Grande Chartreuse in France, which is most well known for its production of Chartreuse, the famous aromatic liqueur. The earliest recorded use of the name Chartreux (spelled with an 'x') was in 1723, when the Universal Dictionary of Commerce in France used this name to describe cats with blue fur. Later, the naturalist Carolus Linneaus (1707–78) recognised the Chartreux as a distinct variety and Georges Louis Leclerc, Comte de Buffon (1707–88) described it as, 'the cat of France' and gave it its own scientific name – *Felis catus cartusianorum*. A lovely description of the Chartreux comes from

the pen of the French writer, Colette (1873–1954), who wrote of her own cat, 'the sun played on her Chartreux coat, mauve and blue like a wood pigeon's neck'.

BLUE CHARTREUX

The Leger sisters from Brittany in northern France were the first fanciers known to have shown Chartreux cats, in Paris in 1931. With a massive body, but with a head that is not so round as the British Blue Shorthair, and a slightly more silvery coat, the Chartreux nearly became extinct after World War II. Today, very few truly pure Chartreux remain in France but the breed was successfully re-established by out crossing survivors with blue Longhairs/Persians (see page 107) and especially, with British Blue Shorthairs (see page 130). For a time FIFé made no distinctions between the Chartreux and British Blue and, in the 1970s, assimilated them into one class under the name 'British Blue'. Today, however, these two breeds are treated as distinct.

The Chartreux is neither cobby nor slender – many cat fanciers describe its conformation as 'primitive', and even as a 'potato on matchsticks' – and its finely boned legs are not thick, although they are short and sturdy and the rounded paws are small in relation to body size. The Chartreux head is a broad trapezoid shape, with a high forehead and rounded-tip ears set high. While the muzzle is narrow, the Chartreux face does

not look pointed because of the rounded whisker pads and quite heavy jowls that become more pronounced with age. The nose leather is a delightful, matching dark blue and the eyes are large, round and copper or gold in colour. To many fanciers of the Chartreux, it is its sweet expression that is irresistible – the Chartreux always seems to have a slight smile! Also intriguing is the naming system for Chartreux cats: each year is assigned a letter – omitting K, Q, W, X, Y and Z – and the cats' names begin with the letter assigned to the year of their birth. Cats born in 2003 will have names beginning with the letter 'U'.

American Wirehair

Date of origin: **1966**

Place of origin: **USA**

Ancestry: **farm cat, American Shorthair**

Other names: **none**

Colours:

Self (solid) and Tortie: **black, red, blue, cream, white (blue-, gold- and odd-eyed), tortoiseshell and blue tortie**

Smoke: **black, red and blue**

Shaded and Tipped: **shaded silver, shade cameo, chinchilla silver and shell cameo**

Tabbies (Classic and mackerel): **brown, red, blue and cream**

Shaded Tabbies: **silver, cameo**

Bicolours: **self and tortie colours with white**

Coat length: **medium**

Type of fur: **springy, tight and frizzy, a bit like lamb's wool, but needs several days to regain curl after getting wet. Curly whiskers**

Size: **3.5–7 kg (8–15 lb)**

BROWN TABBY AMERICAN WIREHAIR

These rare cats are almost unknown outside their native North America, and are one of the very few cat breeds to have truly originated in the USA. The American Wirehair traces its origins back to 1966, when a litter of litters was born to a pair of farm cats called Bootsie and Fluffy, near Vernon, in upper New York state. One of the kittens, a male, had a sparse, very wiry coat. The owners contacted a local breeder John O'Shea, who took the male kitten and one of the 'normal' females from the litter, and began a breeding programme designed to establish the genetic nature of the unusual coat and, if possible, to establish a new breed.

Following tests by geneticists on samples of the hairs, it was discovered that the cat was indeed a completely new type and that it represented a spontaneous mutation whereby each of the longer hairs was crimped and wiry, and bent into a hook at the end. This wiry hair contrasted with other curly-coated cats such as Rexes, whose coats are quite soft to the touch. The American Wirehair it seemed was even more wiry than the Wire-haired Terrier!

AMERICAN WIREHAIR, RED

149

RED AMERICAN WIREHAIR

The original wiry-haired kitten, appropriately called Adam, was a red and white male who, when mature, was mated with its 'normal' litter mate – reputedly a brown tabby and white, but more likely a brown 'torbie' (a brown tabby tortie) – and

their first litter was born on 7 July, 1967. Of the four kittens born, two females were wire-haired red and whites – like dad. One died young, but the surviving female, called Amy, was mated with Adam and went on to give birth to a number of other wire-haired kittens, among them the delightfully named Barberry Ellen, the first homozygous (true breeding) American Wirehair, born in 1969. Adam was also mated to an unrelated short–haired white cat and their litter produced three further wire-haired kittens, thereby establishing the fact that the wirehair gene is inherited in a dominant manner – provided one parent is wirehaired, the litter will contain wire-haired kittens.

Wire-haired kittens are easy to identify at birth: the whiskers and hairs on their faces and ears, as well as those on their coats, are crimped and stick out at different angles. Longer-haired kittens have lovely ringlets, shorter-haired ones have a more wavy appearance. In both instances, however, the coats develop their adult texture in its first year.

The breed standard for the American Wirehair was written in 1967. The CFA requires that all colours, except the silvers, have brilliant golden eyes, although the TICA does not recognise any relationship between eye and coat colour. A rounded head with high cheekbones, a level back and rounded torso, sturdy, medium-length legs with rounded paws and a tapering tail, rounded at the tip but not blunt are defining characteristics of the American Wirehairs conformation. More revealing are the words owners of American Wirehairs use to describe their cats – sinewy, muscular, intelligent and apt to rule the household (and other cats) with 'iron paws', yet at the same time, relaxed, rarely destructive and loving to be handled!

Snowshoe

Date of origin: **1960s**

Place of origin: **USA**

Ancestry: **Siamese, American Shorthair**

Other names: **Silver Laces**

Colours:

    Mitted colours: **seal, chocolate, lilac and blue**

    Bicolours: **mitted colours with white**

Coat length: **short**

Type of fur: **rich and thick. White feet with Siamese-type points**

Size: **2.5–5.5 kg (6–12 lb)**

Named for its characteristic white mittens, the Snowshoe or 'Silver Laces' combines the pointing of the Siamese (see page 161) with white spotting. These beautiful white 'booties' resemble slightly those found on the long-haired Birman (see page 70), but the Snowshoe has a longer head than is considered desirable in a Birman, probably due to the influence of the short-haired breeds that helped to create it.

SEAL POINT AND WHITE SNOWSHOE

SEAL AND WHITE POINT SNOWSHOE

The Snowshoe is the result of efforts on the part of Dorothy Hinds-Daugherty in the 1960s to cross her Siamese with American Shorthairs. At first, other breeders of Siamese cats were suspicious and very cautious of this new hybrid – white toes were a known 'fault' in early Siamese and many feared that the spotting might find its way back into the Siamese bloodlines after many decades of breeding to eradicate it. In fact, the fault may have been inherited from the Siamese's American Shorthair ancestors. Moreover, at the time, the beautiful pointing pattern was the trademark of the Siamese, although today, colour points are recognised in numerous breeds.

The Snowshoe is a moderately sized cat, with what is described as a semi-foreign build – lean yet muscular, somewhere between the muscular cats of northern Europe and the more sinuous cats of Africa and Asia, with a moderately wedge-shaped head, blue eyes and large, pointed ears. It has more oval-shaped paws, with pink and grey paw pads and a long, gently tapering tail. The Snowshoe's coat is short, rich and thick, and lies close to the body.

The mitted pattern is the 'classic' Snowshoe, with the white booties ideally stopping at the ankles on the forelegs and below the hocks on the hind legs. The amount of white must not exceed one-third of the body – except in Seal Bicolour where

BLUE AND WHITE POINT SNOWSHOE

it must not exceed two-thirds of the total body area – with no isolated white spots, although there may be some white on the face. It is, in fact, the facial pattern of the Snowshoe which determines whether a cat is mitted or bicoloured: an inverted 'V' on the nose up between the eyes means a Snowshoe is a bicolour, while anything less makes it mitted. Kittens are born white and it may take up to two years for the markings to be fully defined, with the coloration darkening as the cat matures.

This extremely pretty cat, with a talkative, but soft-voiced nature, remained little known until the 1980s. It was recognised by the TICA in 1983 and though it has deservedly grown in popularity, the Snowshoe still remains rare outside of the US.

Abyssinian

The strikingly beautiful Abyssinian is one of the world's oldest breeds of cat, and one of the world's most popular. The Abyssinian – and its younger, long-haired version, the Somali (see page 100) – are unique in the feline world in that their coat pattern is based on a single mutant gene, not found in any other pure breed. The gene is known as the Abyssinian and denoted, T^a.

Date of origin: **1860s**

Place of origin: **Ethiopia**

Ancestry: **Ethiopian household and street cats**

Other names: **none**

Colours: **names vary internationally**

 Tabbies (ticked): **ruddy (usual), red (sorrel), blue, fawn, lilac (lavender), cream, chocolate tortie, cinnamon tortie, blue tortie, lilac tortie and fawn tortie**

 Silver Tabbies (ticked): **silver, silver sorrel and silver blue**

Coat length: **short**

Type of fur: **glossy and dense, ticked fur colour caused by at least four bands of colour on each shaft of hair**

Size: **4–7.5 kg (9–16 lb)**

BLACK ABYSSINIAN

155

BLUE/SILVER ABYSSINIAN

USUAL COLOUR ABYSSINIAN

The gene is one of the agouti series of alleles and gives each hair several dark bands of colour, which are evenly dispersed on a lighter background. The result is the strikingly beautiful 'ticked' coat pattern, like that of the African Wild Cat. Some residual tabby markings can be found on the head and sometimes on the tail and legs. This breed also has a unique body shape: long, lean, yet powerful and, while it is definitely foreign in body type, it is far less so than the Siamese (see page 161)

Like many of the older cat breeds, the Abyssinian's origins are obscure. Some fanciers trace it back to the Nile valley, as they share a very similar body type to the cats painted and sculpted in ancient Egyptian art. Abyssinians were first brought to Europe in 1868, when a cat called Zula was brought to England by British soldiers returning from the Abyssinian War. It's likely that Zula, along with other imported cats of unknown origin, but with similar markings, were bred as this was a time of great political, economic, cultural and scientific interest in North Africa. These distinctive cats were known by a variety of different names including the 'Hare cat' or 'Rabbit cat', no doubt because its coat was similar to that of a wild rabbit. In France, even today, the

RED ABYSSINIAN

standard Ruddy (as it is called in the USA) or Usual (as it is called in the UK) coat colour – a rich, golden brown ticked with bands of black – is called lièvre, or hare. Genetically, Ruddy/Usual Abyssinians are black cats with the 'ruddiness' due to rufus polygenes. This group of genes modifies the orange colour to produce rich red. They also act on some other pigments to produce the rich colouring of 'show' tabbies and the warm chestnut tone of the Abyssinian.

FAWN/SILVER ABYSSINIAN

Other colours have also occurred in the breed. The Red Abyssinian, now called Sorrel Abyssinian, was recorded in 1887 as coppery-red ticked with light-chocolate brown with the undercoat a warm-apricot. The reason for the name change is because it is now clear that this colour in the Abyssinian is not the result of a true, sex-linked red gene – it's not a true Red at all, but the result of a recessive, light-brown gene (*bl*). The appellation 'Red' is reserved for true sex-linked red-coloured cats as 'true' Red Abyssinians are now bred. A similar name change occurred for Cream

SORRELL SILVER ABYSSINIAN

Abyssinians: the Cream colour was found not to be a true sex-linked cream, but a dilute version of the Sorrel. Cream was renamed Fawn, but then breeders did introduce a true sex-linked Cream – called Cream! In the UK only true reds and true creams are accepted for showings, while some other associations accept these, the Sorrel and Fawn, as well as the other new colours such as chocolate, blue and lilac (a dilute shade of the chocolate).

Accepted as a breed in 1882, Abyssinians almost became extinct in Britain during World War I, but in 1917, the first Abyssinian was registered with the CFA in North America, and by the 1930s, the breed was well established in the USA, where today, it is possibly the most popular breed. It is also one of the most expensive breeds because Abyssinians tend to have small litters – even fewer than other Oriental breeds – averaging about four kittens. Furthermore, it is said that more male Abyssinians are born than females and they mature more slowly than most other breeds, except the Somali, so coat markings may not be evident for some years.

Abyssinians have a very lively and alert appearance. The head is a wedge shape, the eyes are a rounded-almond shape and are green, hazel or amber, rimmed with dark brown or black, with outer, paler 'spectacles' of lighter hair. Sadly these beautiful eyes can suffer from inherited forms of retinal atrophy, a blindness which is more common in dogs than in cats.

FAWN ABYSSINIAN

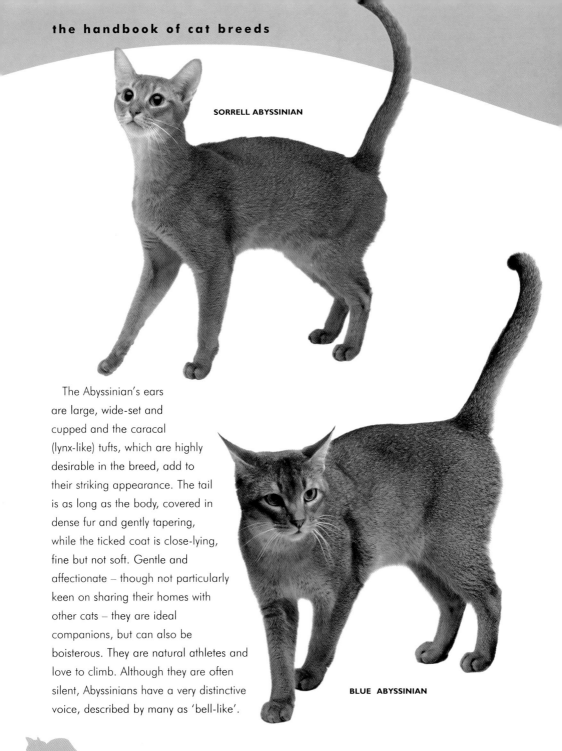

SORRELL ABYSSINIAN

The Abyssinian's ears
are large, wide-set and
cupped and the caracal
(lynx-like) tufts, which are highly
desirable in the breed, add to
their striking appearance. The tail
is as long as the body, covered in
dense fur and gently tapering,
while the ticked coat is close-lying,
fine but not soft. Gentle and
affectionate – though not particularly
keen on sharing their homes with
other cats – they are ideal
companions, but can also be
boisterous. They are natural athletes and
love to climb. Although they are often
silent, Abyssinians have a very distinctive
voice, described by many as 'bell-like'.

BLUE ABYSSINIAN

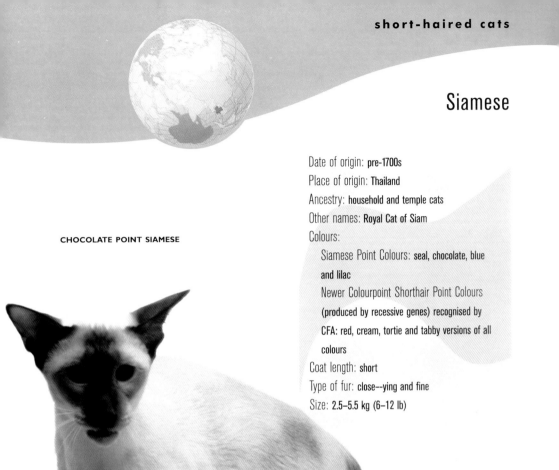

Siamese

CHOCOLATE POINT SIAMESE

Date of origin: **pre-1700s**
Place of origin: **Thailand**
Ancestry: **household and temple cats**
Other names: **Royal Cat of Siam**
Colours:
  Siamese Point Colours: **seal, chocolate, blue and lilac**
  Newer Colourpoint Shorthair Point Colours (produced by recessive genes) recognised by CFA: **red, cream, tortie and tabby versions of all colours**
Coat length: **short**
Type of fur: **close--ying and fine**
Size: **2.5–5.5 kg (6–12 lb)**

161

LILAC POINT SIAMESE

To many people, the Siamese
cat represents the ultimate in
feline beauty and, of all the
breeds, it is probably the most
instantly recognisable with its points – the
coloured ears, mask, 'stockings' and tail –
set against a paler body and offset by
brilliant, piercing, blue eyes. Siamese
kittens, perhaps surprisingly, are white at
birth and only develop their markings and
colour very gradually!

SEAL POINT TABBY SIAMESE

APRICOT POINT SIAMESE

The Siamese is well documented in the art and literature of ancient Siam (now Thailand) and boasts a truly Oriental – and exotic – origin. More than 100 years since it was first introduced to the Western world, the Siamese has remained one of the most popular breeds of both pet and show cat.

There have been many theories as to the origins of the Siamese – including those that say it is related to Egyptian and Manx cats – but it is generally accepted that the Siamese was a variety of cat found in the ancient city of Ayudha, which was founded in 1530 and was Siam's capital until 1767, when the city was invaded by the Burmese. Among the artefacts and manuscripts saved from the city and now housed in the Thai National Library in Bangkok, the most well known – and for many, the most beautiful – is *The Cat-Book Poems*. Its exact date is unknown but it could have been written any time between 1350 and 1750. This manuscript depicts beautiful, pale-coated, seal-point Siamese cats, while the accompanying verses tell of their black tails, feet and ears, and the characteristic

CHOCOLATE TABBY SIAMESE

reddish eye glow of their eyes at night.

These pointed cats were not the only type to be found in Ayudha: other native cats recorded in the manuscripts include the Si-Siwat (see page 192) and the Supalak, but it seems that the pointed cats were particularly valued and were kept in temples and in the royal places. In 1884, the King of Siam gave two Siamese cats to the British Consul-General in Bangkok, whose sister took them back to England to show at the Crystal Palace in 1885. But there are records of Siamese cats in Britain at the first true cat show in 1871 – even though they were described as 'an unnatural nightmare kind of cat'!

When the first Siamese cats arrived in Europe, exotic tales accompanied them – or were invented – to explain their squinting eyes and the kink in their tails. It was said that sacred temple cats were put in charge of the Buddha's sacred vase overnight. In order to make sure nothing happened to it, the cats wrapped their tails hard around the vase and stared at it intently, so that their

tail got bent and their eyes became crossed!
According to another legend, the ladies of
the court entrusted their jewels to their cats
– rings were slipped onto their tails at night
for safe-keeping and the kink developed to
stop them falling off. Scientific explanations
for both the squint and the kink are based
on genetic discoveries. Today, the squint
and kink are considered defects and
through selective breeding, they have largely
been removed from the breed.

In spite of early reactions to the
appearance of the Siamese in 1871, they
soon became a very popular and
desirable breed. They are very
difficult to rear as they are not
the most robust of cats and
are prone to feline enteritis
(a potentially fatal virus
that damages the gut
lining, but which can be
vaccinated against) and
respiratory problems.
But, despite the
difficulties, by the end of
the 19th century, the
Siamese was well established
in Britain and had reached
America in the 1890s.

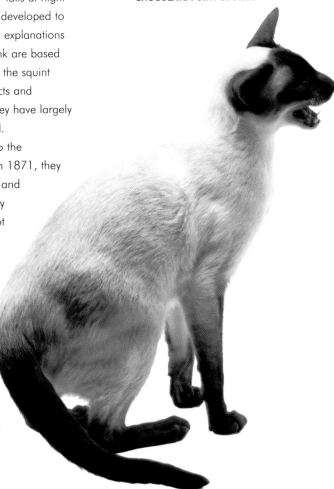

CHOCOLATE POINT SIAMESE

TABBY POINT SIAMESE

The first standards for the breed were written in 1892. Early writers on the breed stated that there were two kinds of Siamese among the early imported cats, but it was the pale-bodied, pointed kind – called the Royal Cat of Siam – that was most highly prized by fanciers. The other type was described as 'chocolate point' – a rich brown colour on the body – with dark points. In 1896, a blue point was exhibited in Britain by a Mr. Spearman, recently home from Siam, but the cat was disqualified by the judge – none other than the famous painter of cats, Louis Wain! Some reports say that this blue-pointed Siamese was a blue self like the Korat (see page 192) but, nevertheless, a blue-pointed Siamese was registered in the late 19th century. By the 1920s, they were appearing in the US where, in 1932, the CFA recognised them, but they were not officially recognised in Britain until 1936. The lilac-point Siamese is the outcome of combining the blue dilution and chocolate-brown genes, and was recognised in the 1950s in the US, and in the 1960s in Britain.

BLUE TORTIE POINT SIAMESE

The quartet of colours – seal, blue, chocolate and lilac-pointed Siamese – are the only varieties regarded as true Siamese by many cat associations. Some purists insist that the only true Siamese is the blue-eyed seal point! Nevertheless, many new colours have been introduced – sometimes classed as Siamese, sometimes as 'Colourpoint Shorthairs'. The first of these colours to become established was the red, followed by tortie points – bred today in seal, blue, chocolate and lilac – and then by cream and tabby point, or lynx point, as it is known in the US. In the 1970s, the discovery of the inhibitor gene (I), responsible for the silver colour in cats, meant that it was possible to breed the Silver Tabby Point Siamese. As a direct result of genetic investigations into cat colours, further varieties were now possible, such as smoke pointed (also known as shadow points), which has heavy tipping on the coloured areas producing a shadowy, tabby pattern – like taffeta or watered silk.

Whatever the colour of their points, all Siamese share the outgoing and vocal characteristics typical of this beautiful breed. Extreme in their looks – their svelte bodies, long heads with slanting eyes and fine muzzles, hind legs longer than their forelegs and long, tapering, kink-free tails – Siamese are also extreme in their character. They are the noisiest, the most boisterous, the most temperamental, the most intelligent and the most demanding cats. But above all, they are the most affectionate cats and, to many fanciers, the most beautiful ever to grace the earth.

In their ancestral home, Siamese cats were never defined solely as those with colour on their points – it was only by chance that the first cats to come from Siam and attract the attention of Western fanciers were pointed.

BLUE TABBY POINT SIAMESE

Burmese: American and European

Date of origin: **1930s**

Place of origin: **Burma (now Myanmar)**

Ancestry: **Temple cats, Siamese crosses**

Other names: **none, but some colours were previously called Malayans**

Colours:

    Sepia American Burmese: **sable, champagne, blue and platinum**

    European Burmese: **self and tortie colours – brown, red, chocolate, blue, lilac, cream, brown tortie, chocolate tortie, blue tortie and lilac tortie**

Coat length: **short**

Type of fur: **sleek and satiny**

Size: **3.5–6.5 kg (8–14 lb)**

Sleek and richly coloured, the muscular, yet compact Burmese have been described as 'bricks wrapped in silk'! While brown Burmese cats have lived in Myanmar for several centuries, the Burmese was the first pedigree breed to be developed entirely in the United States and one of the first breeds to undergo comprehensive genetic studies.

LILAC TORTIE BURMESE

BROWN TORTIE BURMESE

Since it was first introduced to the West in 1930 the Burmese has developed into two types – almost two separate breeds – on either side of the Atlantic Ocean, although the European Burmese is descended from American cats imported into Europe after World War II.

European or American, virtually all modern pedigree Burmese can trace their ancestry back to a single female called Wong Mau. She was an attractive walnut-brown cat, with discernible darker points, taken from Rangoon to the US by US Navy psychiatrist, Joseph Thompson. At the time, no similar cats were known.

CHOCOLATE TORTIE BURMESE

BLUE BURMESE

'All-over-brown Siamese' cats had been seen at 19th century cat shows and similar cats were recorded in ancient Thai manuscripts, but these could have been Burmese or Burmese-Siamese hybrids.

Since there were no other similar cats to mate with Wong Mau, Thompson bred her with a cat of the closest breed – a Siamese – and followed with crosses between the offspring and back to Wong Mau herself. Over the course of several generations, three types of kittens were found in Wong Mau's descendants: those with typical Siamese colouring, those like Wong Mau herself and those which were brown all over – the first true Burmese. Further breeding experiments finally established the existence of the Burmese gene (c^b) and all Burmese cats are homozygous for this – they will breed true. Cats like Wong Mau with intermediate colouring have one Burmese gene and one Siamese gene, and such cats are now being deliberately bred as the Tonkinese (see page 198).

The show standards for Burmese in North America and those in Europe – as well as in South Africa, Australia and New Zealand – are different. The European-Burmese standard considers an oriental, moderately wedge-shaped head, oval eyes and long legs as the ideal. In contrast, the American-Burmese standard favours a well rounded head shape with rounded eyes. This look, however, has brought with it an inherited

CREAM BURMESE

deformity of the skull that can be lethal, often requiring such unfortunate cats to be put to sleep.

In all Burmese, the short, dense glossy coat, which is fine and shiny in texture, is a marked feature and all agree that brown – known in North America as sable – is the primary colour of the breed. There are other colours though, which for some time were classed as Malayans by the CFA. Such colours are blue, where the coat is a beautiful soft, silver grey, shading slightly to the belly with a distinctive sheen on the rounded parts, chocolate (known in the US as champagne) and its dilute form, lilac (or platinum in the US). It is difficult to tell a lilac from a chocolate until kittens are a few weeks old, since both are almost white when born.

A second group of colours includes reds, creams and tortoiseshells, which are based on the orange gene (O) and developed mainly by British breeders in the mid

1970s. The red in Burmese came from three sources: a short-haired ginger tabby, a red-point Siamese and a tortie-and-white farm cat. From these lines a breeding programme evolved to produce clear, red or cream coats, as free from tabby markings and bars as possible. The reds in Burmese are lighter than other reds and often described as 'tangerine', with darker ears, pink nose and paw pads. Creams are rich with only slightly darker ears, while tortoiseshells, which are invariably females, can be dramatically blotched with very attractive facial blazes and solid areas of light or dark colour allowed. Generally though, Burmese tend to have smaller colour patterns than other tortoiseshells. Although not all colours and patterns are recognised by all associations – some insist that only the brown and blue are the real thing – the Burmese is among the most varied in colour of the pedigree cat breeds.

BROWN BURMESE

Whatever disagreement exists regarding colours, there is complete consensus about the personality of the Burmese. Strong and athletic, fearless and fun, affectionate and intriguing, they will live happily in the town or country. Despite the relatively high proportion of congenital (inborn) skull abnormalities – possibly due to inbreeding during the early years of the breed's development – most Burmese cats live healthy and long lives (18 years and more are quite usual!)

Savannah

Only since 2002 has the F_3 (third generation) of this new breed been accepted with experimental status by the TICA only.

The Savannah is a new cat breed – in many instances still in the early 'experimental' stages of development. It was developed as a hybrid of domestic cats and African Serval cats (*Felis serval*), a long limbed African cat with a tawny coat spotted with black, about 60 cm (24 in) at the shoulder, and about 1.5 m (5 ft) from nose to tail tip. Because the domestic cat and the Serval Cat are two different species, successful matings of this kind are difficult to achieve, so consequently, Savannah cats are still extremely rare. The Serval Cat's gestation period is 74 days; a domestic cat's is around 65 days. The difference in these two periods has led to premature births and stillborn offspring.

In appearance, the Savannah is a small 'replica' of its wild ancestor, but still larger than an average domestic cat. The first three generation of Savannahs, were called F_1, F_2 and F_3 respectively: these offspring had a spotted coat pattern identical to the Serval, but with varied background

Date of origin: **1990s**
Place of origin: **USA**
Ancestry: **African Serval Cats and Bengals**
Other names: **Savana**
Colours: **Varied**
Coat length: **short**
Type of fur: **varied from coarse to fine**
Size: **Up to 76 cm (30 in) from nose to tip of tail, 8–13 kg (18–29 lb)**

SAVANNAH

175

SAVANNAH

colours. At the moment the only colour variations that are permitted are gold to orange ground colours with bold, black markings; silver ground with bold black markings, and black smoke. Additionally, the coat textures can vary from the coarser texture of the Serval coat, to the denser, softer and smoother coat of the domestic cat.

Some breeders are using Bengals (see page 218), which are also spotted, in their breeding programmes in order to maintain and enhance the spotted coat pattern, and in the expectation that, with each successive generation, the Savannah will 'shrink' in size, until they are about the same size as the average domestic cat. The first three generations (F_1, F_2 and F_3) of males were expected to be sterile, and the females to be fertile. The rare examples of Savannahs show this new breed to be a very distinctive

and beautiful cat: lean and muscular, with long slender legs and small feet with long toes, the Savannah has a tail that is three-quarters the length of the average domestic cat's tail. When alert the Savannah's tail is held curled up and back a little over the rump. The body is long, almost 'Oriental' but much more massive; the neck is sleek, the ears large and round. The slightly oval-slightly almond-shaped eyes are rich yellow, green, golden or a caramel brown and there are black 'tear drops' at the inner eyes.

In character Savannahs are described as 'dog-like' – they do like to be at the centre of activity, but like all cats, they also enjoy climbing and perching in high up places where they can watch the world go by! Although they remain rare, the Savannah is fortunately displaying 'hybrid vigour': a strong and disease-resistant constitution. Coupled with their distinctive good looks, the Savannah seems set to become a firm favourite with cat lovers.

Chausie

The Chausie is one of the most recent cat breeds – its foundation was registered with the TICA only in July of 1995 – and was originally a hybrid of the African Jungle Cat (*Felis chaus*) and the domestic cat. The African Jungle Cat is also known as the Swamp or Reed Cat and is native to Egypt and South Asia where, as it names imply, it can be found living in marsh and scrubby grasslands. The Jungle Cat is one of the larger of the small wild cats, and weighs on average between 7 and 16 kg (16–35 lb).

The Chausie is recognised provisionally by the TICA in three colours of their short, close lying coats – all of which are the same as those found in the wild Jungle Cat: black, black with silver ticking, and golden, which ranges from a ruddy colour (similar to the Abyssinian's colour, see page 155) to a light, reddy-fawn. As kittens, Chausies commonly display stripes or spots, but as they mature, these fade to leave a beautiful ticked coat, which ideally has between three and seven 'bars' of colour on each hair. In adult cats, bars or stripes on the legs remain visible.

The head is a moderate wedge shape, with a square muzzle and round whisker pads; the eyes are large and angle slightly towards the lower edge of the moderately large ears.(Ear tufts, like those of its wild

Date of origin: **1990s**
Place of origin: **USA**
Ancestry: **African Jungle Cat (*Felis chaus*) and domestic cats**
Other names: **none**
Colours: **black, black with silver ticking, golden**
Coat length: **short**
Type of Fur: **close lying**
Size: **35.5–45.7 cm at the shoulders (14–18 in), 8–13 kg (18–29 lb)**
The Chausie is currently not recognised by the CFA, and has provisional acceptance by the TICA.

BROWN TICKED TABBY CHAUSIE

BROWN TICKED TABBY CHAUSIE

The Chausie is becoming famous for its speed and athleticism: they are capable of jumping vertically to heights of nearly 2 m (6 ft), and their long hind legs make them capable of quite a speed! With a rectangular-shaped body, a full, broad chest and strong bones, ideally, the Chausie should be twice as long as it is tall. Consequently, this large cat is often twice as tall as the average domestic cat and can be up to three times as heavy!

In spite of their size and recent wild origins, Chausies are sweet-natured and affectionate cats that are also very loyal to their owners. They have been described as 'dog-like' in their behaviour – perhaps because of their loyalty and devotion, and the fact that they are also highly intelligent: they enjoy fetching toys when they are tossed! However, they are certainly cats in their curiosity and their habits of enjoying a climb along the mantelpiece, sitting on shelves, and lying in warm places, such as on top of the computer!

ancestor, are highly desirable in a Chausie). Yellow and gold are the preferred eye colours, but hazel is also acceptable. A distinctive feature of the Chausie is its relatively short tail: only three-quarters of the natural tail length of the domestic cat, the Chausie's tail extends to just past the hock (heel) on the hind leg. This feature is due to a recessive gene: artificial 'docking' of the tail is not permitted in the breed.

Burmilla (Asian Group)

Date of origin: **1981**

Place of origin: **Britain**

Ancestry: **Burmese, Chinchilla Longhair/Persian**

Other names: **Burmilla**

Colours:

CHOCOLATE SHADED SILVER BURMILLA

Burmilla or Shaded (Solid, Sepia): **black, chocolate, red, blue, lilac, cream, caramel, apricot, tortoiseshell, chocolate tortie, blue tortie, lilac tortie and caramel tortie**

Silver Shaded: **colours and patterns as for shaded**

Smoke (solid, sepia): **as for shaded**

Self (solid) bombay (ie. black but not to be **confused with the breed of same name, see page 183): chocolate, red, blue, lilac, cream, caramel, apricot, tortoiseshell, chocolate tortie, blue tortie, lilac tortie and sepia colours**

Tabby (all patterns in solid, sepia): **brown, chocolate, red, blue, lilac, cream, caramel, apricot, tortoiseshell, chocolate tortie, blue tortie, lilac tortie and caramel tortie**

Silver tabbies: **colours and patterns as for standard tabbies**

Coat length: **short**

Type of fur: **fine, soft and dense, and close-lying**

Size: **4–7 kg (9–15 lb)**

The Asian Group of cats, also known as the Burmilla, is a Burmese-Chinchilla Longhair/Persian (see page 107) cross and is the result of a chance mating between a Lilac Burmese queen and a Chinchilla tom in London in 1981. Their offspring of four were very attractive, silver-shaded kittens and were the founders of the breed. In 1984 the Burmilla Cat Club was founded and following consultations with the various cat-fancy organisations, a breeding programme was established.

The original litter were of the Burmese type and, initially, the policy was to breed Burmillas to Burmese mates at every other generation in order to enlarge the genetic base. Although the Burmilla shares essentially the same origins as the long-haired Tiffanie (see page 104), in 1989 the beautiful Burmilla was recognised by the GCCF – and, in 1994, by FIFé – as sufficiently distinct in breeding to designate them as a group, rather than a breed, and the Asian Group had the first breed standards that allowed points to be awarded for temperament. Consequently, the Burmilla is set to become increasingly popular not only because of its good looks but also for its extremely good nature, which makes it an ideal household pet.

The most striking features of the Burmilla are their dark 'eyeliner' and the way that their nose pads – which are a lovely terracotta red rather than pink – are also outlined, making these cats look as if they have enjoyed a full beauty and make-up treatment. Their magnificent eyes are half way between round and almond-shaped

LILAC SHADED SILVER BURMILLA

and a delightful green. Burmillas have strong bodies, with a gently rounded head and quite large ears that are set wide apart and angled slightly outwards. Their legs are a medium length – the hind legs are slightly longer than the forelegs – with oval-shaped paws and black paw pads.

A long tail that tapers to a rounded tip is usually carried elegantly, slightly up. Their coats are short and fine, but also very soft and dense, the fur lying close to their bodies.

The Burmilla, or Asian Group, includes shaded and tipped cats, but their coats should not be so lightly tipped that it appears white. Tabby markings are restricted to the 'M' mark on the face, legs and tail, and the 'necklaces' – rings around the neck – must be broken. Ticked tabbies are allowed in both standard and silvered coats in all the Asian colours. Although the intensity of colour may be reduced in silver tabbies, there should always be at least two bands of darker ticking on each hair.

The original self colour of the Burmilla, is the 'Bombay' – a sleek black. This colour name must not be confused with the Bombay breed (see page 183), which stands alone as both a breed and type of cat.

Bombay

Named after the Indian city where black leopards, or panthers, are still to be found, the Bombay was the result of American breeder Nikki Horner's attempts in the 1950s to create a 'mini black panther'. By the 1960s, Horner had produced the first of these glossy, black-coated, muscular cats with rounded heads and brilliant copper-coloured eyes. Although Bombays are

Date of origin: **1960s**
Place of origin: **USA**
Ancestry: **Sable Burmese and black American Shorthairs**
Other names: **none, but often described as 'mini black panthers'**
Colours:
　Self (solid) colours: **black**
Coat length: **short**
Type of fur: **thick and glossy, like patent leather!**
Size: **2.5–5 kg (6–11 lb)**

similar to Burmese, they are not simply black Burmese cats: Bombays were produced by a mating with a black American Shorthair (see page 138) and a sable (brown) Burmese (see page 170).

The resulting offspring, having only one Burmese gene (c^b) were black, but had the silky, short coat of the breed. Because the sepia-pointing gene of the Burmese is recessive, sable kittens with sepia pointing, still sometimes appear in Bombay litters and all Bombay kittens have tabby

BLACK BOMBAY

markings at birth! The full luxurious depth and colour of the Bombay can take up to two years to develop fully.

As a breed, the Bombay was slow to be recognised, but in 1976, it was accepted for championship status by the CFA and, since then, the Bombay has changed its appearance from that of its Burmese ancestors. The Burmese heritage meant that some Bombay lines suffered the congenital skull deformities and breeding to avoid this has meant that the Bombay's head is now closer to that of the American Shorthair (see page 138). The face is a moderate wedge-shape, and the nose leather, paw pads and eye rims are solid black (or a very, very dark brown). The largish ears have rounded tips and tilt forwards very slightly, giving the Bombay the impression that it is always listening intently to what you are saying! The long tail is carried proudly, the back is straight and the body muscular – and surprisingly heavy. Bombays have rather voracious appetites and while they can grow into quite large adults, they never lose their natural gracefulness.

Highly affectionate, the Bombay, like the Burmese, is best described as a 'heat seeking' cat – it adores the warmth and consequently will sit happily for hours (or days if given the opportunity) on someone's lap, having their coats stroked to maintain the sheen and texture.

SELF BLACK BOMBAY

Havana

Date of origin: 1952

Place of origin: USA and Britain

Ancestry: chocolate–point Siamese and Russian Blue

Other names: none, but see text

Colours: chocolate brown is standard, but frost (lilac) cats occur

Coat length: very short

Type of fur: dense and glossy, close-lying and no markings

Size: 2.5–4.5 kg (6–10 lb)

HAVANA KITTEN

The poets of ancient Siam (Thailand) treasured all-brown cats. Considered to be of great beauty, they protected their owners from evil. Such cats were among the first Siamese to arrive in the West in the 19th century. It now

COLOUR HAVANA

appears likely that there were in fact, several distinct genetic types among these cats including what we would now call Burmese (see page 170) and Tonkinese (see page 198), as well as self chocolates. In the early 20th century, the Siamese Cat Club in Britain ruled that it would only encourage the breeding of the blue-eyed Siamese cats that are typical of the breed today and the few all-browns remained in obscurity until the 1950s.

Two breeders in Britain began working to breed solid-brown cats with the chocolate colouring of Siamese rather than the sable colour of the newly imported Burmese. At this time, the only recognised foreign breeds – other than Siamese – were the Russian Blue (see page 189) and the Abyssinian (see page 155). The first kitten of the new colour was born in 1952 and was the result of a cross between a Seal Point Siamese (carrying the chocolate-brown gene) and a short-haired black cat (itself produced by crossing a seal point with a black cat). This became the foundation of the new breed of elegant and graceful cats that was originally registered in Britain as Chestnut Brown Foreign Shorthair in 1958.

Around the same time, a pair of Chestnut Brown Foreign Shorthairs were taken to the United States to establish the breed in America, and here they were registered as Havanas – named not after the Cuban city, but after the breed of rabbits of the same colour! In 1959, the breed was recognised in the US, but was called officially 'Havana Brown'. British 'Chestnuts' continued to be imported into the US and registered as Havana Browns until 1973, when the CFA accepted the Oriental Shorthair breed (see page 203) and, from then on, these imports were registered as Chestnut Oriental Shorthairs. Just to confuse things even more, the Oriental Shorthair colour that is called 'chestnut' in the US is now confusingly called 'Havana' in Britain!

The Havana Brown thus developed as a uniquely North American breed and the standards for judging are different to those in the UK. In the US, breeders prohibited the use of Siamese in the breeding programme and consequently the American cat is a much sturdier animal with a more rounded face and slightly longer fur. In Britain, on the other hand, the emphasis was towards a more Siamese-type body and, consequently, British Havanas are much more vocal than their American counterparts!

In either case, standing high on its legs, with a head slightly longer than it is wide and a distinct 'stop' on the nose just between the oval, chartreuse-green-coloured eyes, the Havana is indeed the rich, dark colour of a very expensive cigar!

Because Russian Blues were used in the breeding programme to create the Havana, the recessive dilute-blue gene was introduced which has led to the occasional appearance of delicately coloured Lilac (Lavender) Havana cats.

Russian Blue

Exotic origins – always attractive in a cat breed – coupled with the most desirable of all the self colours, blue, makes the Russian Blue one of the most magnificent cats. The Blue is the original self colour of the breed and, some say, the only genuine Russian, although black and white forms have been developed recently. The Russians are said to have originated in the White Sea port of Archangel, from where sailors took them to western Europe in the 1860s.

Although Harrison Weir mentions the cats by name in his book *Our Cats* (1893), the Russian Blues were also known by a variety of names: the Archangel Cat, the Spanish Blue and the Maltese Cat. However, from 1917 – the date of the Russian Revolution – until 1948, they were known officially as Foreign Blues.

Date of origin: pre-1800s

Place of origin: believed to be the Russian port of Archangel

Ancestry: domestic cats

Other names: Archangel Cat, Maltese Cat, Spanish Blue, Russian Shorthair, Foreign Blue

Colours: blue, (black and white have been developed and accepted in UK, but not in the USA or by FIFé)

Coat length: short

Type of fur: Double coat with dense undercoat, the plush fur is reminiscent of seal fur

Size: 3–5.5 kg (7–12 lb)

RUSSIAN BLUE

In their early years, at cat shows in Britain, all short-haired blue cats were shown in one class whatever their body-type. Consequently, the Russian Blues competed in the same group as British Shorthairs. The British type – cobby and round headed – invariably won in this class and interest in the finer-boned and narrower-headed Russian breed declined. In 1912, separate classes for British and Russians Blues – still called Foreigns at this time – were established and interest in the Russians flourished once more.

Like many European breeds, the Russian Blues suffered greatly during World War II and, in fact, came dangerously close to extinction. In the late 1940s and early 1950s though, breeders in Scandinavia began developing the breed, crossing a blue cat from Finland with a Siamese carrying the dilution (d) gene which is responsible for the blue colouring. At the same time in Britain, Russian Blue breeders were out crossing to blue-point Siamese and produced cats with a much more pronounced Oriental/Foreign body-type. More recently, breeders have been working to re-create the original features of the breed by crossings with British Blues (see page 130).

The Russian Blue bred true for centuries because the gene responsible for the colour dilution is recessive, never masking any other colours. The newer Russian Blacks and Russian Whites are therefore regarded by many purists as controversial and they are not officially recognised in North America or by FIFé. Most controversial of all are Blue-Pointed Russians, the result of the earlier Siamese out crosses.

The most vivid features of the Russian Blue are its wonderfully thick, lustrous coat and its wonderful emerald-green eyes. The soft, dense double coat, ideal for insulating the body from the icy blasts of a Russian winter, is unique in its feel. The British breed standard describes the coat as 'the truest criterion of the Russian'. The original blue colour is an even blue with a silvery sheen that gives the Russian's coat a luminous appearance. Many breeders claim that the less frequently a Russian is brushed, the more radiant the coat becomes! This is because the coat is 'upstanding' and care must be taken not to polish and flatten it, although the coat of a Russian Blue in tiptop condition will spring up regardless of which way you brush it! The eye colour is more recent in origin: the first Russians exhibited at the Crystal Palace show in England in 1871 had yellow eyes and it was not until 1933 that the breed standards called for them to be as 'vividly green as possible'.

The Russian is a well-muscled cat, but its body is never cobby or heavy. The long legs make for an elegance that belies their sturdiness. The head is a moderate wedge shape and

longer from ears to eyes than from eyes to nose, with prominent whisker pads and large, pointed ears wide-set on the head. Those remarkable eyes are large, almond-shaped and wide-set on the head. Nose and paw pads match the body colour, while the tail tapers to a rounded tip.

Quiet voiced and very non-destructive cats, Russians make ideal house pets, although they can be very offhand with strangers – in most instances they disdainfully ignore them! The reason for this behaviour is that they save all their affection for their owners and each other!

191

Korat

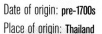

Date of origin: **pre-1700s**

Place of origin: **Thailand**

Ancestry: **household cats**

Other names: **Si-Sawat**

Colours: **blue**

Coat length: **short**

Type of fur: **flat and silky, lacks full undercoat**

Size: **2.5–5 kg (6–11 lb)**

Similar in size and colour to Russian Blues (see page 189) the Korat was known in its native Thailand for centuries as Si-Sawat, which means 'lucky'. Thought to bring prosperity to their owners, they were often given as wedding gifts while, in the rural areas, the 'storm coloured' Korats are reputed to have power over the weather – to encourage rain to fall, farmers were said to pour water over the cats! In the 19th century the Si-Sawat was renamed the Korat by King Rama V, after the remote, high plateau region in north-eastern Siam (now Thailand) where they were believed to have originated.

SILVER BLUE KORAT

In the ancient Thai manuscript, *The Cat-Book Poems*, dating from the Ayutthaya period (1350–1767) these muscular, curved-bodied cats had silver-blue coats described as having 'roots like clouds and tips like silver', and eyes that shine 'like dewdrops on a lotus leaf'.

These manuscripts also show that the Korat today not only has the same beautiful coat texture and colour, but also the same, semi-cobby build evident in Korats centuries ago. In this respect, the Korat is pretty unique since other native Thai breeds, also

represented in these manuscripts, have subsequently been developed by western breeders into cats far-removed in looks from their ancestors.

The first Korats reached Britain about the same time as the Siamese in the late 19th century. In 1896, a Korat was entered in the Siamese class at a National Cat Club show in England, but was disqualified on account of its colour. Some say this cat was a blue-point Siamese, others say it was an all-blue Siamese, but Korats were not registered until 1959, when a pair named Darra and Nara were brought from Bangkok to the United States by Mrs Jean Johnson. The pair were soon joined by more of these delightful cats and, in 1965, a breed club was formed to promote them. By 1969, all the major North American (and Australian and South African) associations recognised the breed. The Korat reached Europe later in 1972, when they were exported from the US to Britain. At first there was some opposition from fanciers who initially felt that the Korat was not especially different from other blue short-haired cats, but by 1975 the breed was recognised in the UK.

Nevertheless, the Korat remains rare – even in its native Thailand. This is because Korat clubs insist that the breed be maintained as a natural breed, so out crossing with other breeds is forbidden. Consequently, all Korats should have an ancestry that can be traced back to the original cats of Thailand as depicted in the ancient art and literature of the country.

The Korat has a delightful heart-shaped head and remarkable, oversized, round, peridot-green eyes, giving it a rather innocent expression – belying the fact that they are notoriously pushy, demanding, stubborn and intent on having their own way! The paws are oval and compact, with dark-blue pads with five toes in front and four at the back. Because of their tropical origins, the Korat lacks a full undercoat and, therefore, must be protected from cold weather. Rarely, some cats suffer from neuromuscular disorders called GM1 and GM2, the presence of which needs to be established by blood tests.

Singapura

The Singapura is the smallest breed of cat in the world – the average cat weighs in at a mere 2.7 kg (6 lb) – and it is also one of the most recent breeds. It takes its name from the Malaysian name for the city of Singapore, which means 'lion-city'. The official mascot of Singapore is a Singapura cat called Kucinta, and there is also a statue of one of the cats on the Singapore River. The original cats of Singapore were nocturnal, feral cats that lived largely in and around the sewers, scavenging for food at

Date of origin: **1975**
Place of origin: **Singapore and the USA**
Ancestry: **disputed**
Other names: **none**
Colours:
Ticked Tabbies: **sepia agouti**
Coat length: **short**
Type of Fur: **sleek**
Size: **2–4 kg (4–9 lb)**

BROWN TICKED SINGAPURA

195

night. These cats were known locally as 'Drain Cats'.

In 1975, two American breeders, Hal and Tommy Meadows, brought cats from Singapore to the United States to originate a breeding programme. All of the cats registered today as Singapuras originate from the Meadows' breeding programme. The Singapura achieved formal championship recognition in 1988, although neither FIFé nor the GCCF recognise it because there are still doubts surrounding the breeds origins. While feral cats from Southeast Asia have been the basis of other breeds such as the Wild Abyssinian, the Meadows were also prominent breeders of both Burmese and Abyssinians and some maintain that these were used in the Singapura's breeding programme, making the feral cats the 'inspiration' for the breed, rather than being the genetic founders of the breed. This view hinges on the fact that the only colour in which the Singapura is bred is Sepia Agouti – a distinctive ticked tabby with at least two bands of ticking on each hair. Genetically, it is a sable ticked tabby, which is the result of combining the Burmese allele (see page 47) with the agouti (tabby) pattern, first known in the Abyssinian (see page 155).

If the Singapura's colour and pattern are derived from Burmese and Abyssinian genes, its size and quiet, retiring temperament are characteristics of its cautious feral ancestors, which attracted little attention to themselves and developed only to a size that can be maintained on a very meagre diet.

The small body of the Singapura is carried on strong, but not stocky legs. The paws are small and oval in shape with brown paw pads and dark hairs between the toes. The head is rounded, with a straight nose and a rather broad, blunt muzzle. Ears are wide and deeply cupped, set slightly outwards – giving the impression that the cat is always listening out for anything sneaking up on them. The almond-shaped eyes are hazel, green or yellow and beautifully outlined in black. From the inner corner of the eyes and running to the whisker pads are dark marks called 'cheetah lines', which are evident even in young kittens.

The Singapura is an extremely rare breed, even in the USA where it was developed, and there are still only some 2,000 Singapuras, making them one of the most valuable breeds.

BROWN TICKED TABBY SINGAPURA

Tonkinese

Date of origin: **1960s**

Place of origin: **USA and Canada**

Ancestry: **Burmese and Siamese**

Other names: **once known as the Golden Siamese**

Colours:

Self (solid) colours and Tortie Mink: **brown (called natural mink in US), chocolate (honey mink in US), blue (blue mink in US), lilac (champagne mink in US), red, cream (both not universally recognised in the US), brown tortie, chocolate tortie, blue tortie, and lilac tortie**

   Tabbies (all patterns): **colours as for self and torties**

Coat length: **medium-short**

Type of fur: **soft, thick and close-lying, with a natural sheen – often described as being like a 'mink coat'**

Size: **2.5–5.5 kg (6–12 lb)**

'Tonkinese' is the new name for an old breed – the ancient 'Copper Cat' of Siam (Thailand). The coppery-brown cats of ancient Siam were known as the Supalak, or Thong Daeng and were illustrated in the manuscript called *The Cat-Book Poems* created by artists and poets in the old capital of Ayudha between 1350 and 1767. The Supalak are now considered to be the ancestors of the Burmese (see page 170) and also the Havana (see page 185) and the Tonkinese itself is a cross between the Burmese and Siamese.

APRICOT POINT TONKINESE

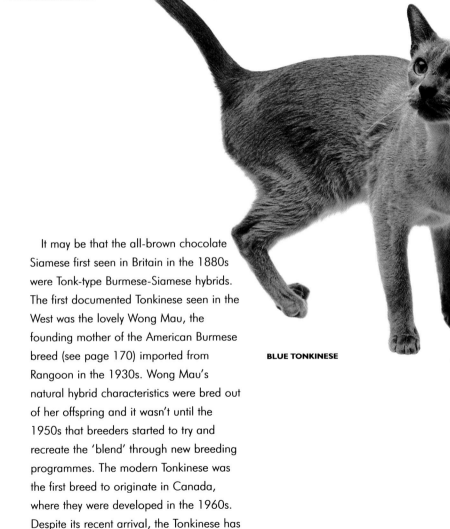

BLUE TONKINESE

It may be that the all-brown chocolate Siamese first seen in Britain in the 1880s were Tonk-type Burmese-Siamese hybrids. The first documented Tonkinese seen in the West was the lovely Wong Mau, the founding mother of the American Burmese breed (see page 170) imported from Rangoon in the 1930s. Wong Mau's natural hybrid characteristics were bred out of her offspring and it wasn't until the 1950s that breeders started to try and recreate the 'blend' through new breeding programmes. The modern Tonkinese was the first breed to originate in Canada, where they were developed in the 1960s. Despite its recent arrival, the Tonkinese has already proven to be one of the most popular breeds.

RED TONKINESE KITTEN

Tonks carry one Siamese (c^S) gene and one Burmese (c^b) gene and its physical features represent a beautiful blend of its two parent breeds – less angular and sleek than the Siamese, but strong and quite heavy, like the Burmese, with a personality that has the lively and affectionate nature of all Oriental breeds.

A Siamese-Burmese cross produces all-Tonkinese kittens, but mating two Tonks will produce on average, two Tonk kittens and two other kittens – one with Burmese and one with Siamese colourings. Because of the slight differences in the European Burmese and the American Burmese, European Tonks tend to be slightly more angular than their North American counterparts.

LILAC TORTIE TONKINESE

BROWN TORTIE TONKINESE

The Tonkinese was first recognised by the Canadian Cat Association and given championship status in 1984. Not surprisingly, soon after, these attractive and friendly cats were accepted by all the major registries. There is, however, considerable variation in the colours accepted and even in the names of colours!

The colour known in the US as 'Natural', is known everywhere else as Brown. It is a light brown, halfway between the Burmese 'sable' colouring and the Siamese 'seal' colouring with darker seal points merging gently into the body colour. The eye colour in Naturals is blue-green. The Lilac – known in the US as Champagne – is a pale, dove grey with a pinkish-coloured cast, with the points a darker shade of the

LILAC MINK TONKINESE

RED TONKINESE

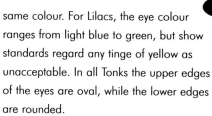

same colour. For Lilacs, the eye colour ranges from light blue to green, but show standards regard any tinge of yellow as unacceptable. In all Tonks the upper edges of the eyes are oval, while the lower edges are rounded.

Red and Cream Tonks may show slight tabby markings – these are very difficult to eliminate in all breeds in these colours – but both Red and Cream Tonks, while recognised in UK standards, are not universally recognised in the US. In Torties and Tabby Tonks, the pointing is much less apparent because it is overlaid with the coat patterns, but the masks and legs should still be darker than the body. The Tonkinese varieties are known as 'Mink' because the Tonk's coats are so remarkably soft and dense and have an exceptional sheen. This coat can take up to two years to develop to its full beauty.

CHAMPAGNE MINK TONKINESE

Oriental Shorthair

Date of origin: **1950s**

Place of origin: **Britain**

Ancestry: **Siamese, Korat, Longhairs/Persians, Shorthairs**

Other names: **in Britain, they were previously known as Foreign Shorthairs**

Colours:

Self (solid) and Tortie colours: **black, havana (chestnut brown in the US), cinnamon, red, blue, lilac, fawn, cream, caramel, apricot, 'Foreign White' (in UK), oriental white (US), black tortie, chocolate tortie, cinnamon tortie, blue tortie, lilac tortie, fawn tortie and caramel tortie**

Shaded, Smoke, Tipped: **colours as for self colours and torties, except white**

Tabby (all patterns) and Silver Tabbies (all patterns): **colours as for self colours and torties**

Coat length: **short**

Type of fur: **close-lying, fine and very glossy**

Size: **4–6.5 kg (9–14 lb)**

BLUE ORIENTAL SHORTHAIR

203

BLACK ORIENTAL SHORTHAIR

In spite of the name – and their beautiful exotic looks – Oriental Shorthairs, which were formerly known as 'Foreign Shorthairs' in the UK, do not necessarily come from the East! The name, in fact, refers to breeds that have a slender physique, a pointed head and slanted eyes. In other words, these Oriental Shorthairs are Siamese cats, but without the colourpoint markings. In the ancient manuscript, *The Cat-Book Poems*, the ancestors of modern brown and blue breeds, as well as black, white, black and white bicolour (called the Singhasep) and shaded silvers were all depicted. Even today in Thailand, it is estimated that in the Bangkok area, only some 20% of 'Siamese' cats are pointed, and the rest are self or selfs-with-white.

CHOCOLATE TORTIE SHORTHAIR

After the Siamese Cat Club of Britain ruled that it would only encourage the breeding of the blue-eyed pointed Siamese, self cats with yellow or green eyes were excluded from the Siamese classes at shows. While this marked a period of initial decline in the excluded cats, it also marked the beginnings of a new chapter in the history of the separate breed of cats now known as Oriental Shorthairs.

The Oriental Shorthair encompasses all cats with the 'Siamese' (i.e. Oriental or Foreign) body shape that are not pointed. Technically, whether self coloured, bicolour, tortoiseshell, tabbies, tipped, smoked or shaded, these cats are all one breed, sharing the elegant, lithe and sinuous body shape, the long expressive tail and narrow, wedge-shaped head.

CINNAMON ORIENTAL SHORTHAIR

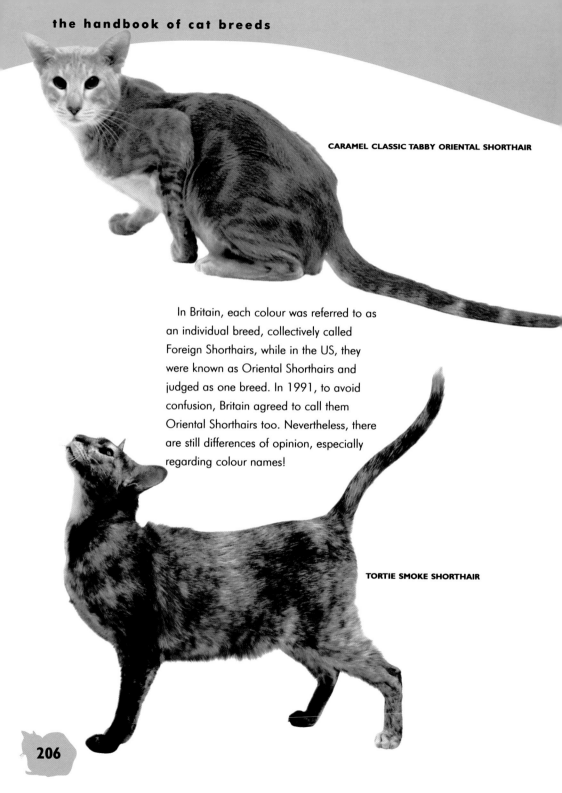

CARAMEL CLASSIC TABBY ORIENTAL SHORTHAIR

In Britain, each colour was referred to as an individual breed, collectively called Foreign Shorthairs, while in the US, they were known as Oriental Shorthairs and judged as one breed. In 1991, to avoid confusion, Britain agreed to call them Oriental Shorthairs too. Nevertheless, there are still differences of opinion, especially regarding colour names!

TORTIE SMOKE SHORTHAIR

WHITE ORIENTAL SHORTHAIR

With the exclusion of all but the blue-eyed pointed Siamese from the show class, interest in the breed as a whole declined, except for all-black and all-blue cats of similar body shape which were being bred in Germany until the outbreak of World War II. It was only after the war that a breeding programme in Britain was planned, the aim of which was to breed all-brown cats with a Foreign/Oriental body shape. The real progress in breeding the modern Orientals began in 1962, when a ten-year programme began to create a breed of true-breeding, blue-eyed, white Oriental cats. These blue-eyed

APRICOT SILVER SPOTTED ORIENTAL SHORTHAIR

CHOCOLATE SILVER SPOTTED ORIENTAL SHORTHAIR

whites were totally different in appearance and character to white cats of other breeds and, significantly, did not suffer any of the problems of deafness associated with the colour. UK show standards require White Orientals to have blue eyes, while in the US and elsewhere, green eyes are also permitted. Because of this difference in standards, in Britain, blue-eyed whites are designated 'Foreign White' while in the US and elsewhere, blue- or green-eyed whites are called 'Oriental Whites'.

RED ORIENTAL SHORTHAIR

Because the white coat of the breed is dominant and masks any underlying colour genes and because to 'fix' the blue eyes and body shape of the Oriental back crosses to pointed Siamese were required, some of the kittens bred in the early Foreign White litters were non-white. Some didn't simply have coloured points, but were coloured all over, and the first of these were solid reds, solid blacks and spotted tabbies. Oriental Spotted Tabbies were once called Maus – but this name was often confused with the Egyptian Mau (see page 211) bred in the US and they were subsequently renamed.

CINNAMON SELF ORIENTAL SHORTHAIR

LILAC ORIENTAL SHORTHAIR

209

Also apparent was one kitten with an obviously Siamese body and a rich chestnut colouring. This colour was first called Havana but was recognised as Chestnut Brown. In 1970 it reverted to being called Havana – but in the US it is still called Chestnut Brown to distinguish it from the separate breed of brown cats called Havana! Siring this chestnut-coloured cat with a lilac-point Siamese, gave the potential to produce cats both of its own rich-brown colour and of lilac – called Lavender in the US!

Other selfs soon followed: the magnificently striking Black Orientals are indeed jet-black, from the tips to the roots of their coats and in their eye rims and paw pads. There are also pale browns, such as Cinnamon and Caramel. The former is a light brown, best described as the colour of milk chocolate, while the latter is often described, equally deliciously, as café au lait. New, gorgeous colours and patterns continue to be produced so that today there are more than 50 recognised.

CARAMEL SILVER SHADED ORIENTAL SHORTHAIR

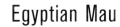

Egyptian Mau

The spotted tabby pattern can be found on a number of breeds of cats, but only one makes any serious claim to be a natural spotted breed rather than the deliberate creation of modern-day breeders. The Egyptian Mau is one breed that closely resembles its ancient ancestors – the common ancestors of all domestic cats. Many examples in ancient Egyptian art depict cats with a colour and coat pattern of spotted tabbies. 'Mau' is an appropriate name for the breed – in Egyptian it means 'cat'!

Date of origin: 1950s
Place of origin: Egypt and Italy
Ancestry: Egyptian street cats, Italian domestic cats
Other names: none
Colours:
Self (solid) colours: black does occur, but not universally accepted
Tabby (Spotted): bronze
Silver Tabby (Spotted): silver (pewter in US)
Smoke: black
Coat length: short
Type of fur: soft and dense
Size: 2.25–5 kg (5–11 lb)

BRONZE EGYPTIAN MAU

SILVER EGYPTIAN MAU

The Egyptian Mau was introduced to the United States in the early 1950s by Russian émigré, Nathalie Troubetskoy who, while in Cairo, Egypt, was captivated by the spotted markings of the street cats which roamed the city. Troubetskoy took a silver-spotted female home with her to Italy where she was mated with a local smoke-spotted tom. The results were bronze-spotted kittens. In 1953, the first pair of Maus, called Gepa and Ludol, reached the US, but it would be another 15 years before the first cat association, the CFF, gave the Mau official recognition and another 10 years before the Mau was recognised in Britain.

The Mau is a svelte cat, medium sized and well muscled, it is neither cobby nor foreign. The face likewise, is neither rounded nor wedge shaped and the nose is the same width from tip to brow. The 'M'

mark is apparent on the forehead, along with an intricate pattern of spots, which have been likened by many fanciers to a scarab beetle. The unusually large, green eyes, which change colour from dark to pale green as the cat matures, are accentuated by very distinctive 'mascara lines'. These wishbone-shaped lines run underneath the eyes from the outer edges of each eye, a bit like Cleopatra's eye make-up as seen in the movies! The most striking parts of their appearance, however, are the spots along the spine running in symmetrical lines and merging into the dorsal stripe at the beginning of the tail, where the sports turn into bands. Although show judges prefer the spots on the flanks to be round and evenly distributed, more often they are random – but no less lovely! The legs too are banded.

The recognised colours in the breed are silver (black spots on a silver agouti background), bronze (chocolate spots on a bronze agouti background) and smoke (black spots on grey, with a silver undercoat). Mau smokes differ from smokes in other breeds because instead of being selfs with no tabby markings, they are distinctly tabbies. The silvery-white undercoat shows just enough to provide contrast and no more. In all colours, gooseberry-green eyes are preferred.

Although they appear to have a worried look – largely due to their large, rounded eyes and their tendency to 'talk to themselves' in a variety of melodious 'chortles' – Maus are very friendly cats, although they can be annoyingly aloof at times!

BLACK SILVER SPOTTED EGYPTIAN MAU

213

Ocicat

Date of origin: **1964**

Place of origin: **USA**

Ancestry: **Siamese, Abyssinian, American Shorthair**

Other names: **Oci**

Colours:

Spotted Tabbies: **tawny (CFA Designation), brown, chocolate, cinnamon, blue, lavender/lilac and fawn**

Silver Tabbies (Spotted): **as for standard tabbies**

Smokes: **as for tabbies**

Self (solid) colours: **as for tabbies**

Coat length: **short**

Type of fur: **soft, fine and sleek**

Size: **2.5–7 kg (6–15 lb)**

SILVER OCICAT

A relatively new breed, the delightfully named and fine-looking Ocicat, is the result of a chance mating between a male Chocolate Point Siamese and a female hybrid – an Abyssinian Seal Point Siamese. The offspring, born in 1964 in Michigan, USA, looked Abyssinian, but when one was bred to a Siamese, the litter included not only Abyssinian-pointed Siamese, but a spotted kitten, called Tonga. At first, this spotted cat was called an 'Accicat' – to describe the accidental ancestry – and then later 'Ocelette' – to describe its similarity to the ocelot. Tonga was neutered and became a much-loved pet, but owner, Virginia Daly, then repeated the mating, producing Dalai Talua, the foundation female of the breed. Tom Brown helped to continue the Ocicat's development, introducing American Shorthairs. In 1966, the Ocicat received its first official recognition from TICA.

TAWNY BROWN OCICAT

CHOCOLATE OCICAT

A rather large breed – they are muscular and surprisingly solidly built cats – an Ocicat averages about 6 kg (13 lb) when fully grown (males are much larger than females). Most outstanding is the Ocicat's rich, 'jungle-like' coat pattern of distinctive spots, the distribution of which should follow the classic tabby pattern, swirling around the centre of their fine flanks.

Originally, these spots were either chestnut-brown on a cream background, or light chocolate on cream, both with golden-yellow eyes. More recently though, silver Ocicats have been developed – the genes coming from American-Shorthair out crosses during the development of the breed. All the silver colours have a white ground, which does much to show off the magnificent markings.

The wedge-shaped head with a broad muzzle makes for a pointed face, enhanced by large, almond-shaped and slightly tilted eyes. Like the Egyptian Mau (see page 211) the Ocicat's eyes – which, according to show standards, must not be blue – are enhanced by dark rims, surrounded by lighter 'spectacles' and wishbone-shaped 'mascara lines' on the temples and cheeks. The tail is long and slender and, like the legs, is banded. But right at the tip is where the coat is most truly shown. While breed standards called for a cat of 'wild' appearance, the Ocicat is graceful, playful and very sociable – as sweet natured as any cat one could ever wish for!

CHOCOLATE SILVER SPOTTED OCICAT

Bengal

Date of origin: **1983**

Place of origin: **USA**

Ancestry: **Asian Leopard Cat, Egyptian Mau, Indian street and household cats**

Other names: **once called Leopardettes**

Colours:

Tabbies (Spotted and Marbled): **brown, charcoal and snow**

Coat length: **medium-short**

Type of fur: **soft and dense**

Size: **5.5–10 kg (12–22 lb)**

**BROWN/BLACK
SPOTTED BENGAL**

Still a rare breed, the Bengal combines the wonderful wild colours and markings of the Asian Leopard Cat with the dependable, trusting nature of the domestic cat. The Asian Leopard Cat is a small wild cat weighing only about 4.5 kg (10 lb) that inhabits the forests of Southern Asia. In the 1960s, there was concern about the possible extinction of the Asian Leopard Cat, which led Jean Sugden (later Mill) of California, in 1963, to attempt to conserve the breed by mating it with domestic cats.

Other wild cats such as ocelots and margays have often found their ways into homes where they have bred successfully with household cats and, in most cases, their offspring have displayed the same temperaments as their wild parent. Ten years later, Dr. Willard Centerwall at the University of California continued the breeding programme while investigating the Asian Leopard Cat's natural immunity to feline leukaemia. From these beginnings, the beautiful Bengal was developed. Dr. Centerwall gave eight of his hybrids to Jean Mill and the first Bengal, called Millwood Finally Found, was registered in 1983.

BROWN MARBLED BENGAL

SNOW-SPOTTED/AOC EYE BENGAL

While early crosses to non-pedigrees introduced some 'undesirable' genes for colour dilution and long hair, later crossings to Indian street cats and Egyptian Maus introduced genes for spotting, the Siamese coat pattern and blue eyes, resulting in the extraordinarily beautiful 'Snow' shades. While breed registries are controlled to avoid unexpected occurrences, Bengal breeders were delighted with the happy accident of introducing pointed lines from non-pedigree cats to create really stunning colours, which are described as a 'pearl dusting' on the coat.

SEAL MINK MARBLE BENGAL

The first coat to be stabilised in the breed was the Brown Spotted and in this pattern, the Bengal closely resembles the Asian Leopard Cat – all the way down to the light-coloured 'ocellus', an eye-like spot as on a peacock's feather on the back of each ear. The markings are deep brown or

SNOW-SPOTTED BENGAL

221

SNOW-MARBLED BLUE-EYED BENGAL

black. The spots on the coat should be large, forming rings or rosettes and randomly distributed. They should not resemble the vertical stripes of a mackerel tabby, which is the underlying pattern to most spotted tabbies. In the Marbled pattern, the coat must not show the blotched or classic tabby pattern and, uniquely, Marbled Bengals, should show three shades of their colour – the base, the dark markings and darker outlines.

As expected from a breed which owns its origins to a small leopard, the Bengal is a very strong cat, with a broad chest, large, rounded paws on strong legs and a muscular neck. The head is a small, rounded wedge with a short nose that is terracotta in colour and outlined in black.

The ears are short, with a wide base and rounded tips, but without ear tufts. Eyes are large, oval and green in colour and are set at a slight slant. Like their wild forebears they are excellent hunters, but are equally at ease in homes as pets. While some say Bengals are still wild at heart and temperamental, others are quick to point out that this can be true of all cats, whatever their breed!

BLACK SPOTTED BENGAL

223

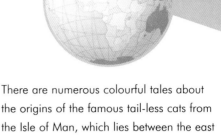

Manx

Date of origin: pre-1700s

Place of origin: Isle of Man, UK

Ancestry: household cats

Other names: none

Colours: Most recognised colours are permitted (see also British Shorthairs, page 130)

Coat length: short, double coat, with thick undercoat and slightly longer overcoat

Type of fur: coarse but glossy

Size: 3.5–5.5 kg (8–12 lb)

There are numerous colourful tales about the origins of the famous tail-less cats from the Isle of Man, which lies between the east coast of Ireland and the west coast of Britain. According to legends, they were the

RED TABBY MANX

last cats to get aboard the Ark and Noah accidentally slammed the door on their tails! Other say Irish invaders took the tails to decorate their war helmets and later mothers bit off their kittens' tails so they couldn't be taken. Some say the Manx cat came aboard Phoenician trading ships 1000 years ago, all the way from Japan – where there are also tail-less cats – and others still, say that they swam ashore from a wrecked ship of the Spanish Armada.

In truth, the isolation of the island allowed an incomplete, dominant gene to become established. The original mutation is thought to have happened some 400 years ago. Spontaneous mutations, such as 'tail-lessness', do occur from time to time in all feline populations but, in large populations, such mutations usually disappear. However, in isolated groups such as the Manx and the Japanese Bobtail, such mutations can survive. Despite being tail-less, the Manx does not suffer from any loss of balance, and is quite good at climbing trees – when the mood takes it!

Manx cats are quite rare; litters are quite small – often only two kittens are born – and this is another result of the Manx gene. Homozygous Manx – those inheriting the Manx gene from both parents – often die in the womb at an early stage of development. The Manx known to cat shows today is heterozygous – it has one gene for tail-lessness and one for a normal tail – but even these show a higher proportion of stillborn and early deaths than most other breeds because the Manx gene can cause malformations in other parts of the body apart from the tail. Spina bifida is quite common and there is often fusion of the bones in the lower spine.

Any cat that is heterozygous can never breed true and, consequently, a number of normal-tailed kittens are likely to be born in any Manx litter. Manx kittens show degrees of variation and these have been divided into four groups for clarity:

'Rumpies', are the true 'exhibition' Manx. They are completely tail-less and have a dimple at the base of the spine; 'Rumpy-Risers' have a small number of tail vertebrae forming a small knob; 'Stumpies' (or sometimes 'Stubbies') have a definite tail stump that is normally moveable and has a curve or kink; 'Longies' have an almost-normal, but truncated tail, which makes them a little difficult to distinguish from 'normal-tailed' cats. Nevertheless, they are all Manx cats since breeders

BROWN TABBY MANX

normally mate Manx with Manx-bred, normal-tailed cats rather than with British or American Shorthairs.

While the missing tail is the most obvious visible characteristic, Manx cats also combine short front legs with longer back legs giving them their equally distinctive 'bunny-hop' gait, known as the 'Manx hop'. Consequently, the Manx's movement is completely unlike the lithe, sinuous movement of other cats. Contributing further to their 'rounded' look, are a round head, full cheeks and a lovely, double coat that shows a well-defined difference

between the soft downy under hair and glossier, but coarser, top coat.

In Britain, the GCCF recognises the Manx in any colour or pattern, while in North America, the CFA excludes varieties that show the effects of chocolate-brown or Siamese genes. While Rumpies alone are show cats, Rumpy-Risers, Stumpies and Longies all make excellent pets with delightful personalities.

American Bobtail

Until recently, there were few tail-less or bobtailed breeds. But both the Manx cat (see page 224) and the Japanese Bobtail have existed for centuries, the latter featuring in ancient prints and paintings as well as on the facade of the Gotokuji Temple in Tokyo, its paw upraised as a symbol of good fortune. More recently, the Kurile Island Bobtail, which hails from a chain of islands running from the easternmost point of the Russian Federation to the tip of Japan's Hokkaido Island, has emerged as a new breed, although it is the product of a recessive gene that is believed to have occurred about 200 years ago.

Date of origin: **1960s**
Place of origin: **USA**
Ancestry: **uncertain**
Other names: **none**
Colours: **All colours and patterns, including sepia, pointed and mink**
Coat length: **short, but long enough to stand away from body**
Type of fur: **slightly shaggy in appearance but does not matt easily**
Size: **3–7 kg (7–15 lb)**

**BLUE LYNX POINT
AMERICAN BOBTAIL**

CHOCOLATE SPOTTED TABBY LONGHAIR AMERICAN BOBTAIL

The American Bobtail is among the first of these new bobtailed breeds. Its origins are obscure – the Bobcat, one of North America's native wild cats, is the only tail-less cat to live on the continent but its part in the parentage of the American Bobtail is unconfirmed. It could also be that Manx (see page 224) and/or Japanese-Bobtail genes may be present since cats of both breeds were popular among breeders in the US. Manx cats appear in early US breed registers and the Japanese Bobtails were first shown in the US in 1963, with the first breeding cats arriving in 1968.

The American Bobtail can only be traced as far back as a random-bred, bob-tailed tabby kitten found on an American-Indian reservation in Arizona, which was adopted and taken home to Iowa by John and Brenda Sanders in the early 1960s. Early breeding work was aiming at producing bob-tailed cats with a pattern like that of the Snowshoe (see page 152), but the cats became unhealthy. Subsequently, breeder Reaha Evans reintroduced more colours and patterns to strengthen the health of the breed which, in 1989, was recognised by the TICA.

There are both long-haired and short-haired American Bobtails, but because the longhair gene is recessive, there are fewer examples of this already rare breed. The short-haired variety, in fact, has a coat whose hairs are long enough to stand away from the body and give the cat a somewhat wild, shaggy appearance. Substantially muscled, the American Bobtail is a semi-cobby cat, with heavy legs and large, rounded paws. Unlike the Rumpie Manx, in the American Bobtail a tail must be present, but should ideally stop short, just above the hock.

SEAL LYNX POINT AMERICAN BOBTAIL

Pixiebob

Date of origin: **1980s**

Place of origin: **USA**

Ancestry: **domestic cats, possible native North American Bobcat**

Other names: **none**

Colours:

Tabbies (Spotted and Rosette): **brown**

Coat length: **short, but long enough to appear shaggy**

Type of fur: **thick and dense**

Size: **4–8 kg (9–18 lb)**

In the past 20 years or so there has been increased interest among breeders in developing new cat breeds by mating domestic cats with wild cat species. In most cases, the offspring inherit the wild temperaments of their ancestors but, in some instances, breeders have made successful crosses with cats such as Geoffroy's Ocelot (*Felis geoffroyi*), a wild cat of the South American upland forests and scrub. Found from Bolivia to Patagonia, the Geoffroy's Ocelot is grey with small, black spots and

BROWN SPOTTED TABBY PIXIEBOB

BROWN TICKED TABBY PIXIEBOB

weighs 2–3 kg (4½–8 lb). When mated with domestic cats, their offspring is a tame cat with the beautiful and exotically spotted coat of the wild cat. Crossing with wild cats such as this, introduces coat patterns not before seen in domestic cats, such as the ocelot-like rosette or ring-shaped spots. Sometimes such cats are called Feral Domestic Hybrid cats, but this is something of a misnomer since the term feral is correctly applied to domestic cats that have 'gone native' and reverted to the wild.

North American breeders have, for some time, been interested in developing a cat that resembles the native tail-less wild cat,

the bobcat. There have been instances of natural matings between wild cats and domestic cats and the origins of the delightful Pixiebob are thought to be the result of such an encounter, although DNA profiles have yet to provide sufficient data to substantiate these origins. In fact, most such kittens have been acquired by breeders from farmers who would otherwise have culled such offspring Two such 'bobcat-to-domestic cat' mated cats were acquired by Carol Ann Brewer in 1985 in Washington State – suitably in bobcat territory! These were then bred to produce Pixie, the founding cat of the breed. Although not known outside of the USA, the Pixiebob was 'allowed' by the TICA in 1995.

In spite of the beautiful wild looks, Pixiebobs are described as having the temperament of a faithful dog! They become very attached to their owners and their homes, and do not readily accept changes to either. Many owners say that they are happiest being the single cat. Their wild looks are enhanced by their wide, round eyes and very strong facial markings – 'mascara' lines on the cheeks and light coloured 'spectacles' around the eyes. Although not essential, caracal, or lynx-like tips on their ears are desirable. But overall, the wild looks of the Pixiebob are in someway mellowed by the delightful, creamy-whiteness of the lips and chin.

BROWN SPOTTED TABBY PIXIEBOB

Cornish Rex

Various rex breeds with short, curly coats have occurred from time to time as a result of spontaneous mutations. They have occurred in Britain, Germany and the US. The degree of curl in rex cats varies from the 'marcel-wave' curl of the Cornish Rex to the 'swirly curls' of the Devon Rex and the 'tufty' curls of the delightfully named La Perm – an American breed developed in Oregon in 1982, which does indeed look like it has a 'permanent-wave' hairdo! In spite of their apparent similarities, these rex cats are distinct breeds: mating a Devon

Date of origin: 1950s
Place of origin: Cornwall, Britain
Ancestry: farm cats
Other names: none
Colours: all colours and patterns including sepia and mink
Coat length: very short
Type of fur: guard hairs are absent, so coat is short, plush and 'rippled'
Size: 2.5–4.5 kg (6–10 lb)

**BROWN MACKEREL
TABBY CORNISH REX**

233

BLACK SMOKE CORNISH REX

Rex with a Cornish Rex will result in kittens with a straight coat, although they will be a little different in texture to that of a 'normal' shorthair.

BLUE AND WHITE CORNISH REX

In 1950, a curly-coated male kitten, called Kallibunker, was born to a farm cat in Cornwall, England. Kallibunker's owner, Nina Ennismore, recognised this curly coat as similar to the rex mutation found in rabbits. By back crossing Kallibunker to his mother, more rex kittens were produced, proving that the rex gene was recessive. In 1957, two of Kallibunker's descendants were sent to the US to found the breed there. Crosses with Oriental Shorthairs and Siamese in the US were called 'Si-rex', while other descendants of Kallibunker were crossed with British Shorthairs and Burmese in Britain.

BLUE CREAM TORTIE CORNISH REX

making the coat soft, short and plush. The waves of curls – which some say look like instant Chinese noodles! – are most evident over the gently arching back and the rump. Because rex cats have finer coats than other short-haired breeds (and the Cornish is completely lacking in guard hairs) they are very sensitive to changes in temperature and need to be kept cosy and warm at all times – just like any other cat, but with an extra special dollop of TLC!

The Cornish Rex has been bred in Britain with a moderately Oriental body type (see page 41), a wedge-shaped head and with what has been described as a 'Roman nose' – straight down from the curved forehead. The ears are quite large and cupped, and are set high on the head, while the small- to medium-sized, well-muscled body is carried high on long and very slender legs – with the hind legs longer than the forelegs. They are famous for jumping and will spend many happy hours leaping from their owner's shoulders onto furniture and back again! British cats are less delicate than their North American counterparts – these have a shape that is a little more like a greyhound, with a more 'tucked up' torso.

What both British- and American-bred Cornish Rexes have in common is the fabulous curly coat. In the Cornish Rex, the guard hairs (see page 42) are absent,

CREAM SMOKE CORNISH REX

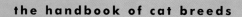

Devon Rex

Date of origin: **1960**

Place of origin: **Devon, Britain**

Ancestry: **feral and household cats**

Other names: **Poodle cats**

Colours: **all colours and patterns including pointed**

Coat length: **very short**

Type of fur: **although Devon Rex have all three types of hair, they are severely distorted, making the coat curly.**

Size: **2.5–4 kg (6–9 lb)**

CREAM SMOKE DEVON REX

CHOCOLATE TORTIE WITH SILVER DARKER POINTS DEVON REX

In 1960, near a disused tin-mine near Buckfastleigh, Devon, England, Beryl Cox found a curly-coated feral cat. A young tortie-and-white stray being cared for by a neighbour mated with this feral cat and, in the resulting litter, was a curly-coated, Black Smoke kitten, named appropriately, Kirlee. The parents of Kirlee were undoubtedly related because the gene for the curly coat is recessive.

CHOCOLATE SILVER TABBY WITH DARKER POINTS DEVON REX

237

BLACK, SMOKE AND WHITE DEVON REX

Because of the earlier publicity surrounding the curly Cornish Rex, which had appeared some 10 years earlier, Beryl Cox was encouraged to breed Kirlee into the Cornish line. To her surprise – and despite several amorous encounters – no curly kittens were born. Only then was it realised that, despite Devon and Cornwall being so close, the two rex cats from these counties carried completely unrelated mutations that would have to be established by separate breeding programmes.

TORTIE DEVON REX

CHOCOLATE SMOKE DEVON REX

BLACK SMOKE DEVON REX

DEVON REX

While the Cornish Rex and Devon Rex both have curly coats, there are significant differences in the breeds. The Devon Rex has an unmistakable head shape that is unique in pedigree cats and is based on the head shape of Kirlee. It's a short wedge-shaped head, with a well defined 'stop' to the nose, large, oval-shaped eyes and prominent whisker pads from which sprout coarsely textured, 'crinkled' whiskers. Furthermore, the Devon Rex has quite enormous ears that are very wide at the base and taper to rounded tips. The effect is a rather pixie or elfin-like face! Facial appearances can be deceptive, however, because the Devon Rex's body, although slender, is solid, hard and muscular! Their

239

WHITE BLUE-EYED DEVON REX

broad chests combined with slender legs – the hind legs are longer than the forelegs – can give them the appearance of being bowlegged, like a feline 'bulldog'!

Unlike the waves of the Cornish Rex coat, the Devon Rex coat is a masterpiece of short, soft rippling and swirling curls and wide out crossings have made for a huge variety of patterns and colours. Most fanciers agree that the curly coat of the Devon Rex will show a Smoke shading far better than any straight-haired cat breed.

BROWN TABBY DEVON REX

240

Sphynx

RED POINT SPHYNX

Date of origin: **1966**
Place of origin: **Ontario, Canada, USA and Europe**
Ancestry: **non-pedigree Longhair/Persian**
Other names: **once called Canadian Hairless**
Colours: **all colours and patterns, including pointed, sepia and mink**
Coat length: **no fur**
Type of fur: **Skin is soft and suede-like**
Size: **3.5–7 kg (8–15 lb)**

For many people the Sphynx is missing the one vital and attractive feature shared by all cats, whatever their pedigree – a furry coat. More or less bald cats, like curly-coated rex cats, have appeared from time to time in various parts of the world. There is some evidence that the Aztecs encouraged hairless cats in their domestic breeds – which may have been destined for human consumption – and for a short time in the 1880s, the Mexican Hairless, was popular.

The 'hairlessness' of the Sphynx is due to a gene. The effects of this gene are incomplete, however, as the Sphynx is not completely hairless – they do have a soft 'peach fuzz' of downy hair. Very thin, very short hairs grow on the ears, muzzle, tail, and feet – and in tom cats, on the testicles.

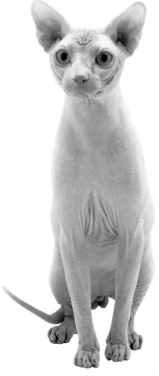

RED MINK AND WHITE SPHYNX

241

LILAC SPHYNX

Each hair follicle has an oil producing gland but, with no real hair as such to absorb it, instead of being combed, Sphynx require a daily rub down with a chamois leather to keep their 'coat' and suede-like skin in tiptop condition.

The first Sphynx – called Prune – was born in 1966, but his line died out. In 1978, a long-haired cat with a hairless kitten were rescued in Toronto, Canada. The 'mutant' kitten was neutered so it could not pass on this 'malformation' but, when the mother had subsequent litters, further hairless kittens were born. Two such kittens were exported to England, where one was mated to a Devon Rex. The result – hairless kittens! That implied that this hairless gene was not only recessive, but dominant over the Devon Rex gene. Further out crossings to Devon Rex were carried out by Vicki and Peter Markstein in New York with their Sphynx, called E.T., but the breed is still rare.

The Sphynx is recognised as a breed only by the TICA as many other organisations still fear there may be potential health risks associated with it. In Britain, Sphynx are registered with the GCCF to make sure that the dominant gene for hairlessness isn't carried into Devon Rex lines.

The influence of the Devon Rex can be seen in the Sphynx's similar 'elfin-like' face with its large eyes and big ears. Their bodies are round and well muscled, with a powerful neck and firm legs. Coat colours and patterns are discernible in the vestigial coat and the underlying skin. In show cats, the 'natural' absence of a coat is vital and any evidence of deliberate hair removal is severely penalised.

While many people find the appearance of the Sphynx 'un-catlike' – they rely on their owners for extra physical protection since their lack of hair makes them very vulnerable both to the cold and to sunlight – in many other respects, the Sphynx is as much a cat as any other. They are affectionate and devoted companions, warm and soft and delightfully playful.

BLUE TORTIE AND WHITE SPHYNX

243

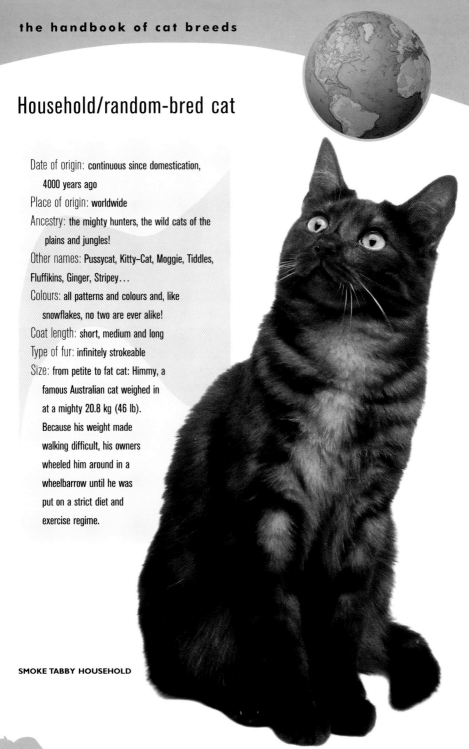

Household/random-bred cat

Date of origin: continuous since domestication, 4000 years ago

Place of origin: worldwide

Ancestry: the mighty hunters, the wild cats of the plains and jungles!

Other names: Pussycat, Kitty–Cat, Moggie, Tiddles, Fluffikins, Ginger, Stripey...

Colours: all patterns and colours and, like snowflakes, no two are ever alike!

Coat length: short, medium and long

Type of fur: infinitely strokeable

Size: from petite to fat cat: Himmy, a famous Australian cat weighed in at a mighty 20.8 kg (46 lb). Because his weight made walking difficult, his owners wheeled him around in a wheelbarrow until he was put on a strict diet and exercise regime.

SMOKE TABBY HOUSEHOLD

With no clubs to promote them or extol their virtues, random-bred cats are nonetheless, the most popular cats worldwide! Random-bred cats live in palaces and small apartments, and are the adored companions of presidents and monarchs, pensioners and children. Sometimes these cats are sociable – they may like other cats and even dogs – other times they are not. Some are talkative, others are silent scrutinisers of the world. Some are 'well-behaved' and others are downright naughty. Some will eat almost anything, others demand a strict gourmet diet!

Whatever their colour, pattern, size or temperament, cats like these have been immortalised in poems, prose, musicals and opera. They have been painted, sculpted and photographed, and have been the stars of movies, cartoons and television adverts.

From home to home and country to country, random-bred cats vary in colour, pattern and size, but each one is still related to the wild cats of America, Europe, Asia and Africa and most random-bred cats will demonstrate this ancestry. Watch them slink as silently as the night through the long grass in the garden! See how they stalk such mighty prey as butterflies! Marvel at their agility as they climb the trees in your neighbours' gardens! Wonder at their mighty roars at night when the big tom from down the road enters their kingdom! And when they're not busy being tigers, you'll find them asleep, curled up or stretched out, in a warm, sunny place – or in the clean laundry basket!

ODD-EYE COLOUR

Pedigree puss or alley cat, in essence, all cats are the same: beautiful, demanding, affectionate, and mysterious creatures deserving of our love and attention to their health and well-being. As the American author Mark Twain wrote,

'A house without a cat, and a well-fed, well-petted, and properly revered cat, may be the perfect house, perhaps, but how can it prove its title?'

Glossary

ACA: American Cat Association, North America's oldest governing body

ACFA: American Cat Fancier's Association

Agouti: The colour between a tabby's stripes

Allele: Any of the genes found at a particular position on a chromosome, which produce alternative physical outcomes. The genes for agouti and non-agouti, and the genes for long or short hair are alleles

Alter: US term for neuter

Awn hairs: Short, coarse hairs lying underneath the cat's top coat

Back crossing: Mating a cat back to one of its parents

Barring: Striped pattern found in tabbies, but considered faults in self (solid coloured) cats

Bicolour: A patched coat of white and another colour

Blaze: A marking down the centre of the forehead

Bloodline: A 'family' or line of cats related by ancestry or pedigree

Blue: Colouring ranging from pale, blue-grey to dark, slate-grey

Breed: A group of cats with similar, defined physical characteristics and related ancestry

Brindling: Scattered 'wrong', or coloured hairs in the coat

Calico: US term for tortoiseshell-and-white patterned cats

Cameo: Coats with red or cream tipping to the hairs

Carpal pads: Pads found above the front feet to help absorb impact on landing

CFA: Cat Fancier's Association, America's largest cat association, also encompassing Canada and Japan

Champagne: US term for the chocolate colour in Burmese (see page 170) and lilac colour in Tonkinese (see page 198)

Chinchilla: Colouring where the outermost tips of the hairs are black, or another colour, with the rest of the hair white or pale

Chocolate: Medium- to pale-brown colour. In Siamese, it's paler than seal

Cobby: One of the body types of the cat – short, compact with broad shoulders and rump, short tail and rounded head

Conformation: Also called 'type' – refers to body size, shape and characteristics of a breed

Cross: Imprecise term for mating two cats and implying that they are distinctly different in colour and/or breed. The term can also be used to describe the offspring of such a mating

Dilute: A paler version of a basic colour such as blue, lilac or cream

Domestic: US term for cats of non-foreign body types, the equivalent of the term 'American' as in American Shorthair (see page 138)

Dominant characteristic: A genetic characteristic passed on to kittens by parents

Double coat: Short, soft undercoat with longer outer coat

Down hairs: Short, soft, secondary hairs

Feral: A domesticated animal that has reverted to, or been born, in the wild. Feral cats are the same species as domestic cats, unlike true wild cats.

FIFé: Fédération International Féline

Flehmen: The facial gesture seen when a cat's Jacobson's organ, in the roof of its mouth, is stimulated

Frost point: US term for lilac (lavender) point

GCCF: Governing Council of the Cat Fancy, the governing body of cat shows in Britain

Guard hairs: Long hairs forming the outer coat

Haw: US term for the nictitating membrane, or 'third eyelid'

Heterozygous: Having one pair of dissimilar alleles – one from each parent – for a particular characteristic

Himalayan patterning: Darker colour at extremities of body, often affected by temperature

Hock: The ankle of a cat's hind leg

Homozygous: Having an identical pair of alleles for a particular characteristic

Honey mink: Intermediate brown colour of Tonkinese (see page 198), corresponding to chocolate in other breeds

Hybrid: The offspring of a cross between parents that are genetically dissimilar – especially between two different species or breeds

In-breeding: Mating closely related cats such as parents to offspring, or brothers to sisters

Jacobson's organ (Vomeronasal organ): A sense organ in the roof of the mouth in cats that responds to chemical stimuli

Kink: Bend in the tail, found in Siamese (see page 161) and other Oriental/Foreign cats

Lavender: US term for lilac

Lilac: Pale, pinkish-grey colour, known in US as lavender

Litter: Kittens born in a single birth

Longhair: Long–haired cats, called Persian cats in the US (see page 107)

Lynx point: US term for tabby point

Mask: The darker coloured areas of the face as seen in Siamese and Himalayan (Colourpoint Longhairs)

Masking (epistasis): The effect that some genes have to conceal or 'mask' the presence of other genes

Mittens: White fur on front feet, as in the Snowshoe (see page 152)

Moggie: Slang word for mongrel, random-bred cat – of mixed or unknown parentage

Moult: Shedding of fur, usually a seasonal occurrence, but common in Longhairs/Persians when stroked

Mutation: Genetic change causing a difference in appearance from parents

Muzzle: The nose and jaws

Natural mink: The darkest colour of the Tonkinese, corresponding to seal-point Siamese and brown (sable in US) Burmese

Nictitating membrane: The 'third eyelid'. Also called a haw in the US

Nose leather: The skin of the nose pad

Odd-eyed: Having eyes of different colours, usually one blue and one orange/copper

Oriental: A term used interchangeably with 'Foreign', refers to body type, especially the extreme body type of the Oriental Shorthair (see page 203)

Pads: Cushions without fur on underside of cats' feet

Papillae: Tiny hooks on cats' tongues which give it its roughness

Pedigree: The line of descent of a pure-bred animal, or the document recording it

Pewter: The British term for Shaded Silver

Pinna: The ear flap

Platinum: The US term for a lilac (lavender) Burmese (see page 170)

Points: The extremities of a cat's body – the head, ears, tail and feet – which are coloured in Siamese (see page 161) and other breeds

Polydactyl: Having more than the usual number of toes

Queen: An un-neutered female cat, especially one kept for breeding

Rangy: A cat with long slender legs

Recessive gene: A gene passed from generation to generation, but not always with visible results

Recognition: The acceptance of a new breed, colour or coat pattern of cat by an association, under each association's rules

Roman: Describes a nose with a high, prominent bridge seen in some Siamese

Sable: US term for brown, the darkest coat colour, in Burmese (see page 170)

Scarab marking: 'M' shaped mark on forehead of tabbies

Seal: The dark-brown colour found at the points of the darkest variety of Siamese

Selective breeding: Breeding by planned mating between individual cats with certain characteristics, which breeders wish to perpetuate or enhance

Self: (in US called solid) having a coat of a single, uniform colour

Shaded: Colouring where the tips of the hairs are coloured, the rest being white or pale, the tipping being part way between the chinchilla and the smoke

Show standard: A description of the 'ideal' cat of a particular breed against which actual cats are judged

Silver: Term applied to shaded silver and silver tabby, both tipped colourings

Smoke: Where most of the hairs are coloured but the roots are white or pale

Solid: US term for self-coloured cats

Spotting: White patches in the coat

Stifle: Cat's knee joint on hind leg

Stop: An abrupt change in the slope of the nose profile

Tabby: A coat marking which can be striped, spotted, blotched or full agouti

Tabby Tortoiseshell: A tortoiseshell cat with tabby rather than self (solid) black patching, also called patched tabby or torbie

TICA: The Independent Cat Association (USA)

Ticking: Bands of colour on each hair, seen characteristically on the Abyssinian's coat (see page 155)

Tipped: The ends of the hairs have coloured tips. The degree of colour or tipping decides whether a cat is a chinchilla, shaded or smoke.

Tom: Un-neutered male cat

Torbie: A tortoiseshell tabby cat

Tortie: Shortened term for Tortoiseshell

True breeding: Homozygous for traits being considered. Such a cat, if mated with a similar cat, will produce offspring like itself which, if in bred, will produce more offspring with exactly the same traits

Type: Overall size and shape of a cat

Van pattern: Bicolour, in which most of body is white, with colouring restricted to extremities

Variety: Strictly, a subdivision of a breed, such as particular colour form. However, sometimes the term is used interchangeably with the term 'breed'

Vibrissae: Whiskers

Wedge shape: The shape of Siamese and other Oriental/Foreign cats' heads

Addresses

Governing Council of the
Associated Cat Clubs of
South Africa
c/o Mrs. M. Simpson,
45 Edison Drive,
Meadowridge 7800,
South Africa

Co-ordinating Cat Council
of Australia (CCCofA)
Box No 4317 GPO,
Sydney,
NSW 2001,
Australia

New Zealand Cat Fancy Inc
PO Box 3167,
Richmond, Nelson,
New Zealand

Fédération Internationale
Féline (FIFé)
Boerhaavelaan 23,
NO–5644 BB Eindhoven,
Netherlands

UK

Royal Society for the
Prevention of Cruelty to
Animals (RSPCA)
The Manor House,
Horsham, Sussex,
RH12 1HG

Cats Protection League
29 Church Street,
Slough,
Berkshire,
SL1 1PW

Governing Council of the
Cat Fancy (GCCF)
4–6 Penel Orlieu,
Bridgwater,
Somerset,
TA6 3PG

Cat Association of Britain
(CA)
Mill House,
Letcombe Regis,
Oxfordshire
OX12 9JD

USA

American Society for the
Prevention of Cruelty to
Animals (ASPCA)
441 East 92nd St.,
New York,
NY 10028

American Cat Association
(ACA)
8101 Katherine Drive,
Panorama City,
CA 91402

American Cat Fancier's
Association (ACFA)
PO Box 203,
Point Lookout,
MO 65726

Cat Fancier's Federation
(CFF)
9509 Montgomery Road,
Cinncinatti,
OH 45242

Index

Bibliography

George MacBeth and Martin Booth (eds), *The Book of Cats* (Penguin, 1979)

Grace Pond (ed), *The Complete Cat Encyclopedia* (Heinemann, 1972)

Grace Pond and Muriel Calder, *The Longhaired Cat* (B.T Batsford, 1974)

Alison Ashford and Grace Pond, *Abyssinian and Turkish Cats* (J.Gifford, 1972)

Mary Dunnill, *The Siamese Cat Owners' Encyclopedia* (Pelham Books, 1974)

Michael W. Fox, *Understanding Your Cat* (Bantam Books, 1977)

Howard Loxton, *Cats:From Family Pets to Pedigrees* (Sundial, 1979)

Michael Wright and Sally Walters, *The Book of the Cat* (Pan Books, 1990)

Collins Gem Cats (Harper-Collins, 1999)

Dr. Bruce Fogle, *Cats* (Dorling Kindersley, 2000)

Credits and acknowledgements

With thanks to:
Vic Swift at the British Library, London and to all the cat owners, breed clubs and societies who kindly shared their knowledge and information on the internet.

Find out more about the different breeds, clubs and societies and about caring for your cats by looking on the internet. If you are considering a cat as a pet make sure you are fully committed to it's care before you take one home: a cat or any other animal – is for life.